Man In Command

*How To Be A Great Husband
and Dad*

Dr. Judith Rolfs

Wayne Rolfs

Dedication

To Chester Vandy and Virgil Rolfs,
dads who recognized the importance of family
and left a legacy of unconditional love
that we're privileged to pass on.

DR. BILL BRIGHT'S ENDORSEMENT OF MAN IN COMMAND:

"MEN ARE RESPONSIBLE for a healthy marriage and happy family. This book can help men fulfill their important biblical responsibilities and avoid stress in the family. Dr. Bill Bright, Founder and President of Cru (Crusade for Christ International.)

This is a week-by-week walk in obedience to the Lord Jesus Christ. Focus on one new way each week to accomplish His goals for your life!"

TABLE OF CONTENTS

INTRODUCTION

The Bible's practical spiritual and emotional lessons can help men in everyday family experiences. Men can model these scriptural principles for their children. Today many men haven't learned these principles and don't know how to live by God's Word. Broken promises and loss of credibility characterize their lives.

Man in Command, How To Be A Great Husband and Dad will help every man be a great husband and dad. The strategies include enjoying and finding satisfaction in these roles. Of course, the 52 ways written here will not create a flawless person—that's God's job. God is the expert, but He has given clear directions and specific principles found in His Word.

God blesses the nation and the men who will courageously live by His Word. If men don't personally guide their children, the powerful forces of the media and peer culture will take over the job. May you commit yourself to be a *Man in Command*—for yourself, your spouse, your children, and for the Lord!

#1 Being An Encourager

Suppose your wife prepares a special meal, but you don't particularly care for it. What if your son strikes out in a baseball game instead of hitting a home run? Are you able to affirm their efforts anyway and help family members feel valued and significant regardless of whether they succeed at tasks or please you in the moment?

Encouragement, men, is the grease that lubricates the wheel bearings of life. The members of your family need your support no matter how well or poorly they perform a task.

How much of an encourager are you? Even though common sense tells you that nagging is wrong, do you tend to harp on some characteristic of your wife or child that irritates you? It's easy to slide into nagging by continually dwelling on minor faults. This deeply injures your wife or child's emotional and spiritual well-being.

Of course you need to teach your children a good work ethic and create high personal standards.

Kids should be clean and well groomed to start the day. Children need to be courteous to family as well as friends. These practices are a necessary part of training little ones. Beyond that, however, there are gray areas that are open to choice. You need to avoid nagging about issues of personal preference.

Wayne discovered he was nagging rather than encouraging when he kept reminding our teenage son David that he wasn't weight lifting enough. Once, twice, three times a night, Wayne would ask David if he'd worked with the weights yet. David finally told his dad how much he hated his constant picking and how he'd lost any desire to exercise. Rather than constantly nagging, it would have been far better for Wayne to pump iron with David and spend the time encouraging him.

The fact is, nagging can't produce the level of perfection we desire in our marriages and in our kids. Constantly noting imperfections leads to discouragement or even despair. It's a sure way to sabotage emotional and spiritual growth.

Often what you perceive to be a fault is merely a personality difference or an interest preference. Your child may not be as outgoing or as driven as you'd like but may be responding appropriately—just differently than you would. For example, some children are naturally more relaxed and slow moving. It does no good for you to prod them to hurry up. In fact, it creates a harmful tension contrary to their innate makeup.

Our youngest child, Dan, moved at a slow pace but always did an excellent job in a reasonable amount of time. Because of his highly organized nature, he planned his work rather than plunging into it haphazardly. Wayne appreciated Dan's work style and encouraged him in his work at his pace. This is the kind of patience and encouragement the heavenly Father models for us.

The key is to identify and praise your wife's and your children's strengths. Your encouragement strengthens the ability of your family members to cope and be productive despite minor human imperfections. Accept their uniqueness. Be very cautious in criticizing minor habits or styles of personality. You want to help them flourish under your encouragement into the people God wants them to be.

Exploring Scripture

Psalm 138:8 says, "The LORD will perfect that which concerns me; Your mercy, O LORD, endures forever; do not forsake the works of Your hands."

According to this verse, who is responsible for perfecting your child? The LORD! You train, He perfects.

Ephesians 4:15–16 says, "Speaking the truth in love, may grow up in all things into Him who the head—Christ—from whom the whole body, joined and knit together by what every joint supplies, according to the effective working by which every part does its share, causes growth of the body for the edifying of itself in love." What does this say about each person's uniqueness?

For In-Depth Study

Read Jesus' parable about the sower in Luke 8:4–15. Verse 15 reads, "But the ones that fell on the good ground are those who, having heard the word with a noble and good heart, keep it and bear fruit with patience." Note that patience is required for bearing fruit. Nothing in life will help you to grow in patience as much as raising a child!

The Christian renewal and transformation process is life long. Romans 12:2 says, "And do not be conformed to this world, but be transformed by the renewing of your mind, that you may prove what is that good and acceptable and perfect will of God."

- Is this transforming process always easy or sometimes painful?

Taking Action

- In what ways have you nagged your wife or children? List something about which you've been too critical.

- How can you be more of an encourager? Write down something you really like about each of them. Is there something you already know they're working hard to change? Try to think of a specific way you can be an encourager.

#2 Telling the Truth

Have you ever been at a social gathering with your family where you gave the phony appearance of having a good time while in fact you couldn't wait to get away from an obnoxious conversation? When you got in the car to go home, perhaps you muttered, "Am I glad to be out of there! I thought that guy would never stop talking." What does that say to your kids, sitting in the back seat? It's okay to pretend? To be a phony? To endure the rudeness or self-centeredness of others?

What if your children heard you interrupt someone politely and say, "Sam, I was wondering what you think about such and such (to change the subject)." Or simply, "Would you please excuse me?" Then (politely) walk away.

One of my counseling clients was careful to always avoid major lies or cheating. He struggled with smaller issues, however, like telling the kids to lie and say that he wasn't home when he didn't want to be disturbed by a phone call. Sometimes he'd fail to correct someone when they paid him an undeserved compliment giving him credit for something he hadn't done.

These two common traps trip up many otherwise honest men:

- Giving a false impression either through what you say or doesn't say.

- Believing white lies are okay if lying is used to protect someone's feelings.

When your family knows you lie, even if it's over small matters, maybe even to spare their feelings, you deny them the chance to trust you deeply. Lying may display a lack of confidence in their ability to deal with an unpleasant reality or your inability to face a situation and become strengthened in the process. In reality, lying demonstrates you're not as concerned for others as you are for yourself. You're simply taking the easy way out. Your children will likely pick up these negative traits and reflect the same behavior.

The question of protecting the feelings of others is a tricky area. Some men assume that hurting someone's feelings must be avoided at all costs. Protecting someone's feelings is never more important than keeping God's commandments. Often important personal growth occurs when someone tell us the truth about ourselves on an issue of significance and vice versa. You can be brave and honest with others.

Joe, a twenty-eight-year-old, unmarried man, was deeply hurt while a young person in his parents' home because of their bad habit of constantly putting him down. Yet even as an adult he couldn't bring himself to confront them for fear he'd hurt them or be totally rejected forever. Instead, he shoved his frustrations down with food—lots of it—and soon weighed over three hundred pounds. His weight became another topic for family put-downs. Joe endured great emotional pain. Yet he heard his brother and sister speak honestly to his parents if there was a disagreement, and his parents accepted it fine.

Since Joe couldn't speak the truth to his parents about his feelings he chose to pretend not to mind being their scapegoat. He came into the office because even eating his way up to three hundred pounds couldn't stop the gnawing pain of his emotional turmoil. He went away sad and unhealed emotionally because he refused to confront his parents kindly and he also refused to forgive them.

This example clearly shows the importance of letting your children know they can share hurts and joys honestly with you, even if they see you as part of the problem. For your family members to be honest in all their social contacts you must demonstrate honesty consistently.

Exploring Scripture

Psalm 15 gives a model for truthful behavior:

"LORD, who may abide in Your tabernacle?
Who may dwell in Your holy hill?
He who walks uprightly,
And works righteousness,
And speaks the truth in his heart;
He who does not backbite with his tongue,
Nor does evil to his neighbor,
Nor does he take up a reproach against his friend;
In whose eyes a vile person is despised,
But he honors those who fear the LORD;
He who swears to his own hurt and does not change;
He who does not put out his money at usury,
Nor does he take a bribe against the innocent.
He who does these things shall never be moved."

- What requirements for truthfulness are described in this psalm?

Jesus is our model. Jesus had a direct and guileless way of communicating with others that was always balanced by compassion. He didn't beat around the bush. Jesus called Judas a devil

(John 6:10), and He labeled the Pharisees as whitewashed tombs. Yet He spoke gently to a woman accused of adultery and accepted social outcasts without putting them down.

Taking Action

• Think about a time this past year when you found telling the truth difficult.

Consider the following statements and mark them True or False.

- True or False - Truth is a precious commodity growing more and more rare.

- True or False -The truth is to be told lovingly, kindly, and consistently at all times.

• Ask God to reveal any instances of lying you need to confess. Write down three specific areas in which you want to practice more truthful communication and share these with someone who will hold you accountable.

#3 Eliminating Secret Sins

A secret sin is any thought or behavior that is contrary to God's principles. It's a thought, word or deed that you'd be ashamed of in the presence of Jesus Christ, and that only you (and God!) know about. Secret sins, whether cheating your employer, abusing drugs or alcohol, fantasizing about sexual affairs, being unforgiving, or harboring bitterness—will often cause you to break your promises of fidelity and integrity. Human pride can make you want to present an image of perfection, so it's often tempting to cover up sin in any area of your life.

A secret sin that frequently traps Christian men today is pornography, "the lust of the eyes." A man may try to justify his actions by thinking pornography will make him more sexually responsive to his wife. What it actually does is stimulate fantasy sex and further isolate men emotionally and spiritually from their wives.

Whatever the secret sin, Satan desires to convince you either that:

- You're not that bad and don't need to change your ways and ask forgiveness. "You're not the only one doing this." or

- You're so bad that it's unspeakable to mention your sin because no one would ever forgive you.

For years Matt struggled with wandering eyes. He said, "I thought everyone liked to look at nice-looking women, and I saw no harm in it—except I knew Jackie, my wife, didn't like it. She felt it was unflattering to her when I stared at someone else. She became very uncomfortable. I'd persuaded her that the problem was her jealousy and insecurity. I was just admiring an 'objet d'art.'

Matt finally admitted that this wasn't proper behavior for a happily married man. He learned not to look twice at attractive women which might lead him to lustful thoughts. His wife Jackie began to feel more secure in his love when he eliminated this practice." Matt finally learned not to tolerate his sin. It didn't happen overnight; it was a long, hard struggle.

Perhaps you've been able to hide a secret sin for some time. It's rare, however, to hide sin over a long period of time. The effects of sin are apt to appear in some way—either physically, emotionally, or spiritually.

A mom brought her ten-year-old girl for counseling. The girl was experiencing feelings of fear and confusion regarding her dad's alcoholism, which he thought he had hidden completely from her. She desperately wanted to talk to her dad about his drinking but was afraid what his reaction would be. Instead, the daughter became extremely anxious and "irrationally" fearful. The root of the problem, however, was her father's alcoholism. As so often happens in families, a child acts out some disturbed emotional behavior that is actually caused by the dysfunction of a parent.

Men, you don't need to act defensively about your shortcomings. Admit it when you forgot to do something or when you should have handled a problem differently. Pretending to be perfect causes your children to think that they have to be perfect. You'll lift an unrealistic burden from your sons' and daughters' shoulders when you free them from the burdens of pretending to be or actually trying to be perfect!

Be unmerciful with yourself is in admitting and confessing sin. Stamp it out. Confessing sin frees you to keep your promises to God and to your family. Your wife and children will feel far more secure in your home if they know you're working to overcome a bad habit or area of sin than if you're trying to ignore and hide it. How about asking for their prayers and their encouragement?

Exploring Scripture

Psalm 19:12 says, "Who can understand his errors? Cleanse me from secret faults."

- What should be our attitude toward secret sins?

Ephesians 5:11–13 has the answer. "And have no fellowship with the unfruitful works of darkness, but rather expose them. For it is shameful even to speak of those things, which are done by them in secret. But all things that are exposed are made manifest by the light, for whatever makes manifest is light."

- Should areas of sinfulness or imperfections be hidden from view until resolved and eliminated?

"Therefore having these promises, beloved, let us cleanse ourselves from all filthiness of the flesh and spirit, perfecting holiness in the fear of God" (2 Corinthians 7:1).

- What do we gain when we free ourselves from secret sins? (Notice this is an ongoing process.)

First Corinthians 6:19 says, "Or do you not know that your body is the temple of the Holy Spirit who is in you, whom you have from God, and you are not your own?"

- How does this apply to secret sin?

For In-Depth Study

Meditate on Psalm 51:1–17, a powerful prayer of repentance.

"Have mercy upon me, O God,
According to Your lovingkindness;
According to the multitude of Your tender mercies,
Blot out my transgressions.
Wash me thoroughly from my iniquity,
And cleanse me from my sin.
For I acknowledge my transgressions,
And my sin is always before me.
Against You, You only, have I sinned,
And done this evil in Your sight—
That You may be found just when you speak,
And blameless when You judge.
Behold, I was brought forth in iniquity,
And in sin my mother conceived me.
Behold, You desire truth in the inward parts,
And in the hidden part You will make me to know wisdom.
Purge me with hyssop, and I shall be clean;
Wash me, and I shall be whiter that snow.
Make me hear joy and gladness,
That the bones you have broken may rejoice.
Hide Your face from my sins,
And blot out all my iniquities.

Create in me a clean heart, O God,
And renew a steadfast spirit within me.
Do not cast me away from Your presence,
And do not take Your Holy Spirit from me.
Restore to me the joy of Your salvation,
And uphold me by Your generous Spirit.
Then I will teach transgressors Your ways,
And sinners shall be converted to You.
Deliver me from the guilt of bloodshed, O God,
The God of my salvation,
And my tongue shall sing aloud of Your righteousness.
O Lord, open my lips,
And my mouth shall show forth Your praise.
For You do not desire sacrifice, or else I would give it;
You do not delight in burnt offering.
The sacrifices of God are a broken spirit,
A broken and a contrite heart—
These, O God, You will not despise."

Taking Action

Before you dismiss secret sin too quickly as not applicable to you, prayerfully ask the Holy Spirit to reveal any secret sin He wants eliminated.

- What areas of sinfulness do you need to deal with?

- Have you tried to hide them? How?

- Are you willing to expose them? Why or why not?

- Will you commit yourself to being accountable to two or

three Christians who will pray with and for you regularly and check up on your progress? Record a time and place and people with whom you'll regularly be accountable.

#4 Correcting Constructively

All dads, at one time or another, have to correct a child's behavior. It goes with the territory of parenting. But some fathers may never have learned the correct way to get through to children so their correction works. Here are some ideas.

First, evaluate whether your child is capable of the behavior you're expecting and mature enough to make the desired change. If not, your instructions are a waste of energy and may be demoralizing. Your child's behavior depends on his or her current level of growth and development.

Then decide exactly what behavior you should expect in the situation. When our son was five years old, I tried taking him to do errands with me. He disliked stores, would kind of "space-out" mentally, and end up wandering off. By age eighteen, however, he liked to shop more than me! We cannot demand better behavior than our children are physically and emotionally capable of performing.

Do you consistently model the behavior you're requesting? "Stop bossing your sister (or brother)!" is a frequently heard phrase in many homes. What message is communicated to children, however, when a parent explodes with anger against the other spouse? It's important to convey respect when suggesting a change in behavior, particularly for older children.

Before you punish be sure you have established a relationship of trust with your child so your correction will be viewed as a desire to be helpful and not hurtful. Control your tone of voice—as well choosing as your words very carefully to avoid belittling tendencies that can damage your child's emerging sense of self-esteem.

Give your child an honest compliment first. This can often soften the criticism. Remember, your children naturally are wired to please you, and they dislike being inadequate in your eyes.

Try using phrases like the following:

- "Dad and Mom are pleased with . . . but we're concerned when you . . ."
- "You're doing a fine job with . . . but we'd like you to also learn to . . ."
- "What if you tried . . .?"

Before correcting, examine your motives. Are you being impatient perhaps? Is your real motivation to have the most perfectly controlled child on the block? Is a behavior really wrong or merely inconvenient or embarrassing for you? Think through these issues; then express the desired changes specifically in words that your child can understand.

Don't forget to examine your own disposition. Are you angry? Wait until you calm down. Are you feeling down or put upon from a situation at work?

If you're weary or stressed, you're not in the proper frame of mind to correct someone else; postpone disciplining your child. Thoughtless criticism can damage your child's emerging sense of confidence.

Another thing to consider and guard against: Being in a position to control can make you feel superior, particularly if your work requires taking orders and pleasing others. It's tempting to enjoy bossing someone else around. Taken to extremes, such parenting may enable you to dump your own frustration or anger onto your child, who then becomes your victim.

Beware of criticizing your child in front of other adults in order to impress them with your conscientious parenting. Ideally, correction should not even occur in front of brothers or sisters.

Always avoid being critical of your children for something they didn't know they were supposed to do. If they weren't taught something, they can't be held accountable for not knowing about it!

Exploring Scripture

"A soft answer turns away wrath, but a harsh word stirs up anger. The tongue of the wise uses knowledge rightly, but the mouth of fools pours forth foolishness" (Proverbs 15:1–2). How do these verses relate to the task of correction and discipline as a parent?

Taking Action

- Check for any unresolved anger or bitterness in any of your present relationships that you may unknowingly take out on your child?

- In what way (or ways) is your child behaving appropriately? Give praise.

#5 Showing Love

There are many ways to show love. One is with words and another with appropriate touching - normal, completely healthy human behavior that Jesus modeled for us. Touching ranges from a polite handshake, standard social formality, to hugs and kisses as expressions of caring and closeness.

Touching should be used often to show love, calm fears, and seal commitments to one another. We extend warmth through a hug or a pat on the back. These physical contacts say, "You're a special person to me." Dads, don't be hesitant to touch your children affectionately.

Both little girls and little boys love wrestling with their dads. How does a dad keep this loving, touching relationship alive and healthy when children grow older? He can give a hello hug and a good-bye hug for children and adults in the family of any age! He also gives back scratches and neck massages - thoughtful gestures that say, "I care how you're feeling."

Exploring Scripture

Matthew 9:29 tells us, "Then He [Jesus] touched their eyes, saying, 'According to your faith let it be to you.'" Mark 8:22–25 says,

Then He [Jesus] came to Bethsaida; and they brought a blind man to Him, and begged Him to touch him. So He took the blind man by the hand and led him out of the town. And when He had spit on his eyes and put His hands on him, He asked him if he saw anything. And he looked up and said,

"I see men like trees walking." Then He put His hands on his eyes again and made him look up. And he was restored and saw everyone clearly.

Why was touch such an important part of Jesus' ministry to the hurting?

Taking Action

Jesus touched the blind man's eyes to heal him. There was healing in His touch. There can be emotional healing in your touch as well, Dad. Do your children enjoy being touched by you? Place your hand on your child's head or shoulder often as you pray for him or her. Ask God to heal any hurts he or she may be experiencing.

- Use non-sexual touch to show love to your wife throughout the day.

- Write your children's names and list specific ways that you can show love to each child by appropriate and loving touch.

#6 Developing Your Child's Creativity

God is Creator of the world, and every human being is created in His image. Therefore, each child is endowed with a touch of creativity from the Creator Himself. You can help develop this creativity God has already placed in your children. Dads have a unique opportunity to children loving, individual attention. Traditional schools, which must deal with large numbers of children and often have institutional atmospheres, are not ideal gardens for nurturing creativity in your children. So, dads, the ball is back in the home court!

First, let's consider how creativity develops. While it's a unique and complex activity, creativity is often born from natural curiosity or simple boredom. It occurs when restless, unused mental energy is directed constructively toward new patterns of thought or action.

You can build a little boredom into family life that will stimulate everyone's curiosity. Spend an evening with the TV off. But don't leave a complete vacuum of time—not at first, anyway. Have a plan. Remember, you are teaching inactive brains to think and provider their own stimulation. Your help may be needed for a while.

When our children were elementary school age, we kept a collection called the junk box filled with miscellaneous hardware, packaging materials, discarded kitchen items, food jars, and other odds and ends. We'd bring out our crazy collection occasionally, add some glue and tempera paints, and fool around making cardboard doll furniture for little kids in the neighborhood, crazy gifts for each other, or strange inventions of all sorts.

Here are some creative alternatives for you and the kids:

1. Discuss making something new out of something old. Start by brainstorming silly, off the- wall, impossible ideas until you come up with something fun and workable. Then, try it! Don't worry about results.

2. Make up what-if questions. What-if ideas stretch creativity by making it acceptable to dream up alternatives to the present situation. Strive for different, unusual answers. These questions are great fun in the car on short trips.

3. Leave special-interest magazines lying around the house. You can borrow these magazines from your local library. Sky and Telescope and Popular Mechanics are examples. Don't limit yourself or your child to one area of interest. Read widely to get a glimpse of God's world. Discuss what still needs doing or discovering. Watch for areas of interest that develop in your child and foster them.

Exploring Scripture

Genesis 1:1, 26–28 says: "In the beginning God created the heavens and the earth. . . . Then God said, "Let Us make man in Our image, according to Our likeness; let them have dominion over the fish of the sea, over the birds of the air, and over the cattle, over all the earth and over every creeping thing that creeps on the earth."

So God created man in His own image; in the image of God He created him; male and female He created them. Then God blessed them, and God said to them, "Be fruitful and multiply; fill the earth and subdue it; have dominion over the fish of the sea, over the birds of the air, and over every living thing that moves on the earth."

- What are some unusual or surprising aspects of creation that constantly remind you of God's infinite creativity and even sense of humor?

- What aspects of the heavenly Father's creativity are displayed in the creative play of your children?

Taking Action

- Use your own creative energy to come up with other ways to encourage creativity in your child. List some here.

#7 Using Uncommon Sense

Common sense is great—up to a point! Make sure your child understands the limitations of common sense. Common sense can endanger creativity and intellectual growth. It is useful in its place, but beware of relying totally on common sense. Why?

Common sense says that airplanes are too heavy to fly through the air and the sun must revolve around the earth. Yet neither conclusion is true. Common sense says that belief in the unity of three Persons as one God is irrational, our salvation experience based on one Man's death two thousand years ago is unworkable, and the supernatural gifts of the Spirit in our lives are self-delusions. Yet personal experience coupled with faith and the use of our God-given ability to study and comprehend God's Word enables us to believe these apparently irreconcilable—but true—concepts.

Common sense, when it helps avoid idealistic thinking and naive mistakes is an important part of maturity. It's irresponsible, however, to make decisions based solely upon assumptions, prejudices, and snap judgments—that kind of "intuition" may be common, but it makes no sense! Good decisions require careful and systematic thinking skills, skills you can help your children develop, skills that require uncommon sense!

Thinking Maps

Teach your child how to use "thinking maps." Sit down at the kitchen table some evening. Turn the TV off. Start with one circle in the center of a page with one idea. Connect it with lines to circles that are offshoots of that idea. Then draw offshoots from them, and so on. This will help your child understand the process of thinking, how one idea leads to another and also helps teach problem solving using the same strategy.

Explain to your child that things are not always as they appear, like the sun "moving around the earth." There are limits to what human reason alone can understand. That's why the Bible is important. It's a revelation—it reveals truths that we wouldn't know on our own, like the nature of God and His plan for our lives.

Exploring Scripture

In James 1:5 we read, "If any of you lacks wisdom, let him ask of God, who gives to all liberally and without reproach, and it will be given to him."

What does the Bible say to do when you need insight and wisdom? What situations have you faced that required seeking God's wisdom?

Taking Action

Life isn't always smooth, neat, and orderly. When the unexpected happens or when things don't go according to plan, what do you do?

- Write down a response plan or thinking map that outlines how you think through a problem.

#8 Forgiving Mistakes

Don't you wish you never made mistakes? Don't you wish you could keep your children from making them? We could all simplify our lives if we never made mistakes! Unfortunately, mistakes come along with this precious package called humanness. No one on the face of the earth is immune to that "crawl off and die" feeling that comes over you when you know you've messed up something important.

Our children need to understand that there are two types of mistakes: morally wrong and morally neutral. Morally wrong mistakes, or sins, often bring harmful consequences to self or others even though forgiveness is readily available. Knowing the principles of God's Word can keep your child from making dangerous, morally wrong mistakes and falling into sin. Help your children improve their memory of Scriptures related to God's helpfulness and forgiveness. Using a Bible concordance, list several verses that present God's loving help and forgiveness. If necessary, paraphrase the verse so that it's appropriate for your child's learning level.

A morally neutral mistake doesn't violate a moral principle or bring the harmful consequences of sin. A wrong turn off the highway is morally neutral. Forgetting an appointment (unless it was done on purpose) is not sinful. These mistakes can become opportunities for personal growth.

Throughout history, some of our greatest discoveries have come about because of a mistake in procedures that created new, unseen possibilities—like Sir Arthur Fleming's "accidental" discovery of penicillin from mold growing in a neglected petri dish. A mistake can be a disguised learning tool.

Tell your child not to be afraid of making mistakes. As long as a person is alive, it's natural to make some mistakes—both morally wrong and morally neutral.

When your children make a mistake, be quick to forgive and don't keep dredging up their past failures or poor decisions. One dad admitted his error when his son asked to go to high school early to participate in a before-school prayer event. He chose that moment to point out that the last two Sundays his son hadn't wanted to go to church, so why did he want to go to a prayer meeting at school now? Needless to say, the father discouraged his son in the exact area where the son needed encouragement. Forget the past and focus on building for the future.

Exploring Scripture

First John 1:8–9 says, "If we say that we have no sin, we deceive ourselves, and the truth is not in us. If we confess our sins, He is faithful and just to forgive us our sins and to cleanse us from all unrighteousness."

We need to keep up-to-date with God and confess our mistakes to Him quickly. As one wise Christian counseled, "Keep short accounts with God."

- Are we ever completely free from sin and the need to confess to God and be cleansed?

- Can morally neutral mistakes become occasions for sinful actions? How?

Taking Action

Give an instance from your own life when you've made each type of mistake and how you dealt with them:

1. Morally wrong

2. Morally neutral

#9 Setting Goals

Your children may never know what a goal is unless you teach them. Setting a goal is a lot like making a promise. When you reach the goal, you feel like you've kept a promise! In order to explain goals, Wayne used comparisons relating to sports. In soccer or hockey, the purpose of the game is to achieve as many goals as possible. Unless you can see the target or finish line it's easy to get sidetracked and wander across the field. In the same way, you can achieve your desired life goals by seeking [defining] them and then staying on target until you hit the bull's-eyes.

In life there are different kinds of goals, and they vary in importance. Most important, of course, are the spiritual goals of salvation and then growth in the Christian life. Other goals can be financial, intellectual, social, or sports-related. Every six months or so, sit down with your children individually and come to some mutually agreeable goals appropriate for their ages and levels of development. Write the goals down. Then, take each child alone every few months and discuss his or her progress. Revise the goals as necessary.

Keep the pressure light and, again, make sure the expectations are realistic. This is a great way to show interest in your children's total development. They'll feel your love through it.

When kids reach adolescence, parents often leave behind making charts and filling them in with stars, yet some individuals—even through adulthood—are helped greatly by these motivational tools. Try them out to see how well they work for your family.

Wayne made a weight-lifting chart with his tall, lean sons to help motivate them. It worked in spurts, but it worked better than if they'd done nothing at all.

Exploring Scripture

Philippians 3:12–14 tells us, "Not that I have already attained, or am already perfected; but I press on, that I may lay hold of that for which Christ Jesus has also laid hold of me. Brethren, I do not count myself to have apprehended; but one thing I do, forgetting those things which are behind and reaching forward to those things which are ahead, I press toward the goal for the prize of the upward call of God in Christ Jesus."

- What are the action words in this passage that tell us to keep setting goals that help us mature and grow in Christ?

Taking Action

- What area of your children's development needs an encouragement chart?

- How should this chart be set up?

- Where should it be placed in the house?

- When will you confer with Your children concerning their progress? (Refer to chapter 1, "By Learning to Encourage," and chapter 4, "By Correcting Constructively," for tips on encouraging your children to achieve their goals.)

#10 Not Acting Too Fast

Do it now! HURRY!!! For a limited time only!!!!

A quick-moving, action-oriented person is admired and even highly respected in today's society. Children observe this hurried behavior and are often pressured to act rashly, make up their minds quickly, and not think through all their options. This need to hurry applies to small and large areas of behavior and decision-making, from doing a chore to deciding how to spend money or free time.

One of Wayne's first jobs was washing windows for a hardware store. As a twelve-year-old, he was eager to make the money. He got paid per window and reasoned the faster he worked, the more money he'd make. After several hours the owner informed him he would have to go back and rewash all the windows! His work hadn't been adequate. Rushing didn't pay.

Wayne found that when he acted or decided quickly, it was often in response to the pressure of someone else. He often experienced the hurry-up lifestyle. In a business deal when he would hear someone say, "Are you in or out? I've got to know now!" he's learned to say, "Count me out." Having been burned several times in business and investment decisions when he was impetuous, Wayne doesn't adjust his natural pace to the demanding pace of those around him anymore.

In the Gospels there are many examples of Jesus' unhurried manner. Jesus was never in a hurry—

He took time for little children, He encouraged Mary of Bethany's unhurried worship, and He did not hurry to the tomb of Lazarus. Yet He was on the go constantly and accomplished much in His brief sojourn on earth.

Respect your own natural rhythm, the way you move through life. Some men think and move quickly, and some naturally like a slower pace because of innate personality tendencies.

Dads, help your children to find their optimum pace, too.

Three principles to teach your children that should keep them on track and working at a healthy pace are:

1. Whenever you feel that you must act quickly, slow down, think and plan (except in emergencies, of course).

2. The more important the decision, the slower you need to make it because the more thought it will require.

3. When you act too quickly, it's often in response to the pressure of someone else. Don't let others determine your behavior.

Christians should respond only to the Father's gentle pressure. Children—and adults—often rush an action or a decision when they're feeling unsure. That feeling of uncertainty is so unpleasant that some want to be rid of it immediately. When they are under pressure, it often seems as though any action is better than inaction. Of course, that's not true. Encourage your child to become comfortable with temporary delay or uncertainty.

Exploring Scripture

Take time to pray before taking action. James 1:5 says, "If any of you lacks wisdom, let him ask of God, who gives to all liberally and without reproach, and it will be given to him."

- How will God respond to your prayer?

Taking Action

When did you recently act fast and then regret it later?

- Plan to share that experience with your child and explain the three principles of making sound decisions.

#11 Making Good Decisions

Being a Man in Command goes hand-in-hand with making good decisions. Here are three key decision-making steps to use consistently and teach your children.

1. Make sure all your decisions are consistent with the principles taught in God's Word. This requires spending time reading it to know what it says. You'll find lots of great practical stuff in the book of Proverbs written by the wisest man who ever lived, Solomon. Specifically does the decision violate one of the Ten Commandments or another clear moral directive?

2. Take time to consider opposing thoughts and arguments. The more important the situation, the more information you need to acquire before you decide. Getting input takes time. Don't reject feedback that isn't what you want to hear at the moment.

3. Take time to pray for wisdom before making a final decision. Wait for the leading of the Lord (this may seem like a strong, clear nudge in a certain direction).

Warning! When you try to make any behavior conform to God's way for your life, Satan will pull out all the stops in a last-ditch effort to rush or confuse or stop you. Satan is never pleased when you carefully follow Christ. Christ will have the victory, however, as you or your children continue to respond in obedience with right decisions. If you fail, admit it, ask forgiveness, and point yourself back to the track you know is right. Each time you practice doing what is right according to God's Word, you'll find it's easier to do the right thing in every area of life.

Don't give up trying to please the Lord in every decision. Don't give up no matter what! This basic truth needs repeating— don't give up! Don't even think about it! That's exactly what Satan wants. To be forewarned of Satan's attack is to be forearmed!

Exploring Scripture

Deuteronomy 6:17 tells us, "You shall diligently keep the commandments of the LORD your God, His testimonies, and His statutes which He has commanded you."

- What is the first principle for good decision-making found in this verse?

- Proverbs 11:14 states, "Where there is no counsel, the people fall; But in the multitude of counselors there is safety."

- What is the second principle for good decision-making found in this next verse?

- In Isaiah 55:2–3 we read, "Listen diligently to Me, and eat what is good, and let your soul delight itself in abundance. Incline your ear, and come to Me. Hear, and your soul shall live."

- What is the third principle for good decision-making found here?

- John 14:21 says, "He who has My Commandments and keeps them, it is he who loves Me."

For In-Depth Study

Read Joshua 9:3–25. What happened to Joshua when he made a hasty decision without investigating all the specifics?

Taking Action

- List some upcoming decisions that need to be made in your life:

- How can you use these principles from Scripture to help you make good decisions and avoid stress?

- In what upcoming decisions in your children's lives can you help your children practice decision-making?

#12 Controlling Moods

Moods are an inevitable part of being human. People are often described as being in a good or a bad mood. Moods can change with circumstances, swinging back and forth like a pendulum— sometimes at one end, sometimes the other, or somewhere in between. Some individuals naturally have wider mood swings than others. Some people seem so easygoing that their emotional equilibrium rarely changes.

Depression and negative feelings are often described as a bad mood, but there is a difference. Being in a bad mood occurs to most of us at some time. It's usually a temporary condition based on circumstances like a flat tire, a poor night's sleep, a late airline.

Depression, however, is a serious condition, an emotional and physical state of darkness that can grow worse. Depression lasts longer than a simple bad mood and may be the result of some significant loss or disappointment or may appear without cause. Many people can work themselves free of depression with positive counsel and loving understanding from those around them; others need professional help.

Responding properly to a "bad mood"—your own or someone else's in the family—is critically important (chapter 13 has specific suggestions on shaking off a bad mood). You need to know how to respond in a healthy manner in order to help your children. Children can be taught how to respond so that a bad mood is only a temporary disturbance in a normally even temperament. Here is how:

When a bad mood strikes someone in the family, model patience and understanding. Tell them, "So you're having a tough time today." Acknowledge their reality. Clue the rest of the family to give them time to work this out. Just be patient and try to understand when he or she is unhappy."

Cory's daughter, Tanya, an attractive teen, would occasionally astound her dad with statements like, "I'm ugly. I hate myself." These statements concerned Cory. Usually the next day, sometimes a few days later, Tanya was her bubbly, contented self again. Her dad took special time to share with her about God's unfailing love and acceptance of her just as she was.

Certainly men have bad moods and mood swings, but women and teens are especially vulnerable to highs and lows because of the hormonal changes in their bodies that create these emotional swings. What an opportunity to grow in patience and demonstrate love.

So, why be concerned about mood swings if they're just the result of physical, hormonal changes? Because if not handled properly, bad moods can become long-term states and result in serious depression. Serious depression can lead to thoughts of suicide—a far too prevalent option chosen by young people today. Stay alert to your own moods and those of the people around you.

Exploring Scripture

Jesus, the perfect Man, displayed a wide range of feelings and emotions throughout His ministry on earth. In Mark 3 Jesus healed a man with a withered hand on the Sabbath in the company of hostile Pharisees. Verse 5 says, "And when He had looked around at them with anger, being grieved by the hardness of their hearts, He said to the man, 'Stretch out your hand.'

And he stretched it out, and his hand was restored as whole as the other." Jesus displayed His feelings of anger and grief at the Pharisees. Then He went ahead and healed the man's hand.

In John 15 Jesus spoke of His own intense delight and desired that His disciples experience it, too. Verses 11–12 read, "These things I have spoken to you, that My joy may remain in you, and that your joy may be full."

Bad moods can be brought on by a lack of joy, by worry, fear, or criticism. In dealing with all these varied feelings, Philippians 4:6–7 says, "Be anxious for nothing, but in everything by prayer and supplication, with thanksgiving, let your requests be made known to God; and the peace of God, which surpasses all understanding, will guard your hearts and minds through Christ Jesus."

First Thessalonians 5:16–18 says, "Rejoice always, pray without ceasing, in everything give thanks; for this is the will of God in Christ Jesus for you."

- What actions should you take based on these verses when you're in a bad mood?

For In-Depth Study

King David, the author of many psalms, displayed a wide range of feelings. Read Psalms 34, 42, and 51.

- Describe what they reveal about how David was feeling.

- Did David have any problem identifying or expressing his emotions? Do you?

Taking Action

Are there some people or circumstances in your life who are likely to put you in a bad mood?

- List them here. Pray for these people and for God to bless your interactions.

- What specific actions can you take to change your mood and correct the situation?

#13 Shaking Off A Bad Mood

Bad moods are typically caused by situations like loneliness, lack of adequate sleep, the body's early warning signal of illness, unreasonable or unclear expectations, setting sights on something unattainable, low self-esteem, or a lack of confidence in God to fulfill His promises in our lives.

Here's a list of fifteen ways to shake off a bad mood. Shaking the bad mood and getting back on an even track moves you toward your goal of keeping your promises to God, yourself, and to others! This list is easy to share with and teach to your wife and children.

1. Talk your feelings over with the Lord. He's close by! Write a letter to Him - record your thoughts in a journal or a personal file on your computer. If you don't have a diary, consider starting one to help you see the ups and downs of your feelings.

2. Tell your wife, your parents, or a trusted friend how you're feeling. Listen for their suggestions and welcome their comfort. In talking with children, stress that your child will make decisions as to how he or she will act, but it's helpful to first get suggestions from parents on important issues. We spent many extra hours counseling teenage children at bedtime as we made the rounds from room to room. Bedtime is undoubtedly the best time to be available for sharing confidences.

3. Change the settings you're in the most. Avoid the tendency to vegetate at home. Go to a park, the library, or walk the

dog. New sights in new surroundings can help break the bad mood.

4. Call an old friend or make a new one. Take the first step. Call someone you'd like to know better and tell him so. The old adage, "To have a friend, you must be a friend," is still a super mood enhancer. Reaching out to others takes the focus off yourself and your feelings.

5. Take on a long-term project. Work alone or with your child to build an iceboat or dollhouse or birdhouse. Plant a flower or vegetable garden outdoors in the summer.

6. Do something different and creative either alone, with your wife or parents, or a friend. Try painting with oil or watercolors. Aim to have fun, not to produce a masterpiece.

7. Plan a trip with your family—a day's outing or a lengthy vacation. Study maps. Even if you don't actually go, it's a refreshing change of pace.

8. Clean and organize your surroundings. Yes, surprising as it sounds, lots of clutter around you can be depressing. Wash the car, rearrange something—your wallet, your dresser drawers, the compartments in your car.

9. Let nature nurture you. Lay on the grass or go for a walk in the rain if it's a rainy day that's got you down—walking in the rain can be fun (watch out for thunderstorms with lightning, of course!). Whenever possible, be outdoors so your body can absorb both the sunshine and the beauty of God's creation.

10. If you need a haircut or new clothes, this is a good time to get them. Do something nice for yourself (within reason and your budget).

11. If these superficial methods don't help lift your mood, analyze yourself deeply. Why are you feeling so irritable?

12. Associate with positive people or read an engrossing book with a positive ending. Get involved with someone or something else to keep you from fixating on yourself. You'll look at what's bothering you differently after a social or mental break.

13. Work out regularly. Vigorous exercise makes the brain produce endorphins. Endorphins create a natural, healthy high. When difficulties seem overwhelming and out of control, exercise can give you a sense of wholeness and control over your body.

14. If the bad mood persists, get a medical checkup or locate a professional Christian counselor for a consultation.

15. This last suggestion is the most powerful, but it's so simple that people fail to use it.

Memorize joyful Scriptures like Philippians 4:6–8. "Be anxious for nothing, but in everything by prayer and supplication, with thanksgiving, let your requests be made known to God; and the peace of God, which surpasses all understanding, will guard your hearts and minds through Christ Jesus.

Finally, brethren, whatever things are true, whatever things are noble, whatever things are just, whatever things are pure, whatever things are lovely, whatever things are of good report, if there is any virtue and if there is anything praiseworthy—meditate on these things."

Repeat them when you start feeling down. Remember how mighty and powerful the Word of God is!

Exploring Scripture

When you talk with children who are in a bad mood, Colossians 3:21 tells you to be sensitive. "Fathers, do not provoke your children, lest they become discouraged."

• What are some typical insensitive approaches?

• How can you be more sensitive?

Romans 8:28 says, "And we know that all things work together for good to those who love God, to those who are called according to His purpose."

• What encouragement can you give your child from this verse?

Taking Action

Discuss in advance these helpful approaches for shaking a bad mood. Sit down with your loved one when he or she is in a good mood. Ask which suggestions sound appealing. Note them and try to remember them.

Each of the suggestions above can be adapted for yourself or to the ages of your children.

#14 Developing Compassion for Those with Handicaps

You retard!" "Idiot!" "Run faster, you slow-poke." Children may use put-down phrases without thinking. Sadly some children and adults live with physical limitations every day. When children meet a handicapped person they may be extremely uncomfortable at first. This is because they don't know how to react. Children can be prepared in advance for these encounters and be taught to be compassionate without condescension.

First realize that when your children are around the handicapped, they may experience the following:

- subconscious fear or squeamish feelings that this handicap could happen to them

- a tendency to reject handicapped individuals who obviously are very different from them and their friends

- simple confusion about how to act

Children may erroneously label the handicapped person as inferior. This labeling creates a sense of superiority in non-handicapped children. Often they want to know what's it like to have a physical impairment. They may wonder how the person feels about their handicap.

Should they discuss the disability? Should they avoid the subject until they know one another well? Is a normal friendship possible?

Teach your children that handicapped people have the same feelings everyone else does. They fear rejection, have normal sexual urges, and want to be considered attractive to the opposite sex. The handicapped child may sometimes feel jealous of brothers or sisters who can do things they can't.

Handicapped children need reassurance that they measure up in their parents' eyes. These handicapped youth have had to work through issues about God, His will, His intervention in human lives, bitterness, and anger—questions that many other children don't need to deal with until they're much older.

Dads, remind your children that everyone —the handicapped as well—want to feel accepted by friends. Handicapped children and adults must overcome self-consciousness at being stared at and viewed as different. They yearn be treated normally and accepted as individuals with interests and needs the same as other people.

Handicapped persons enjoy talking about hobbies they have, places they've been, and shopping purchases they've made. They have the same fears as everyone else and the same desires to be respected for who they are and not just for some particular capability.

Speak to your child about this subject and seek to create a compassionate heart. Without this sensitive heart, your child may withdraw from those who are handicapped or different in some way and miss out on great blessings.

Exploring Scripture

Colossians 3:12, 14 says, "Therefore, as the elect of God, holy and beloved, put on tender mercies, kindness, humility, meekness, longsuffering. . . . But above all these things put on love, which is the bond of perfection."

Teach your child that everyone is handicapped in some way. Some handicaps show on the outside, others are hidden on the inside. We all must struggle to make the most of our strengths and gifts and to minimize our weaknesses.

Taking Action

Think of someone you know who is visibly handicapped.

- How do you feel when you are around this person?

- How do you think this person feels when he or she is around you?

- What are some specific actions you can do to be loving and compassionate toward this person?

- What are some specific things you can to do include this person in ordinary daily activities?

#15 Identifying Burnout

The term burnout is part of the jargon of our culture. Men and women have dealt with burnout long before the condition was labeled. Scripture also deals with burnout (that shows how old it is!) but uses another term—"growing weary."

With four children, it seemed like we'd just get one child through a difficult situation to find another child needing extra comfort or support. Sometimes we need time out, not another major crisis.

Wayne would finish a project for his corporate job that required extra long days and weekend work only to come in and find another demanding challenge on his desk. He performed well and was rewarded—with more work to finish in the same number of hours for the same pay. Soon the corporate ladder became the corporate treadmill.

As a golf club pro Wayne has had to deal with continual requests and demands by his members, from the public players, and from a general manager that often left him emotionally and physically exhausted by day's end.

It's true that long-term emotional and physical demands can make you weary. As simple as it all sounds, the cure for burnout is to know what makes you weary, what refreshes you, and how to keep the right balance between the tasks that weary you and those things that refresh you. When Wayne came home rather than be asked how his day was gone, he preferred not to discuss his work until after dinnertime. Later in the evening he might relieve pressure by recapping certain incidents aloud and getting feedback from me. Many nights his mind was cluttered with concerns of the next day, but reading God's Word in the evening always brought him peace for a good night's sleep.

Exploring Scripture

Galatians 6:9 says, "And let us not grow weary while doing good, for in due season we shall reap if we do not lose heart." Second Thessalonians 3:13 says, "But as for you, brethren, do not grow weary in doing good."

- What do these verses tell us about the relationship between spiritual priorities and burnout?

- What are some of the personal rewards ("we shall reap") of not losing heart?

Taking Action

- What specifically makes you weary?

- What refreshes you?

- How can you and your spouse stay balanced and refreshed in the parenting role? In your work?

#16 Avoiding Burnout in Parenting

1. It's important to take good care of yourself so that you can take good care of your family. Here are nine key ways to avoid the burnout problem in the first place!

2. Avoid expecting too much too soon. Be realistic in your expectations. Children need to hear things said over and over again.

3. Realize that you will pour into your children much more than you will receive back from them. That's just the way it is. If you do your job well, your grandchildren will be the beneficiaries.

4. There are times when it may seem as though nothing you do is working and you can't get through. Don't judge by immediate responses. If you're doing what you know is right, keep at it. Ignore the grumbling and discontent.

5. Be ready to adapt when necessary. Parenting involves constant adaptation. Just when you get a handle on the terrible twos, your child outgrows them.

6. Take care of yourself. When the flight attendant on an airplane gives emergency instructions, she tells the passengers to put the oxygen masks on themselves first—before they help someone else. Parents are better able to help their child if they are functioning properly. That applies to every aspect of parenting. Avoid getting physically, emotionally, or spiritually drained.

7. Set aside time each day or week to recharge your emotional batteries. This might include thirty minutes of reading, a walk, other exercise, or a favorite hobby or sport. These activities can help nip burnout before it takes hold.

8. Check your own self-esteem tank regularly. Is it too low? That's when you're hit by the tendency to magnify every fault in your wife or children or friends. Go to Christ for reminders of who you are and who they are—accepted by God, capable in Christ's love, and valued by one another.

9. Refuse thoughts of fear or condemnation if scary thoughts of failure attack you. After you've done your best as a parent, the results might not be what you'd hoped for. Tell yourself the rest is up to God.

10. Laugh, a lot—alone and with your children! It's true that laughter is one of the best medicines.

Exploring Scripture

"There is therefore now no condemnation to those who are in Christ Jesus, who do not walk according to the flesh, but according to the Spirit" (Romans 8:1).

- In what ways is this the "I did my best" verse and now I'm moving on?

Taking Action

- In which key area(s) listed above do you need improvement?

- What necessary changes do you need to make in your routine or relationships?

#17 Nurturing A Healthy Self-Image

Naturally, you want your children to have a healthy self-image. Sure, you've heard the term self-image a lot, but what is it really? And how does it show up in your child?

A good self-image is a balance between knowing you're okay even though you're not perfect and being willing all the while to work on improving yourself. It's normal for everybody to have a blend of good qualities that need to be developed and bad qualities that need to be controlled. Nobody has it all together, and nobody here on earth ever will. Perfection comes in heaven only. Yet God thinks we're acceptable to Him even in our imperfect state. He's committed to work patiently in us and to encourage us in the process of change.

However, in regard to sinfulness, there are no excuses. Teach your children that when they see sin in their lives, they need to confess the sin to God and to any people who are involved, to ask for forgiveness, and to get busy removing it. How? By changing their thinking and their actions.

Children need to understand the most important issue about self-image is to have a Christ like image. What does He think about us? What does He say about us? In Him is the strength of our self-image.

The Bible says that believers are:

- holy
- blameless

- children of the King

- beloved

- redeemed

- precious

And nothing, nothing can ever separate us from the unconditional love of Christ Jesus. That's why we can face the circumstances of life with heads held high. God has given positive self-image to His children to be used to build His kingdom.

Sometimes self-image is misjudged. Often what appears to be a poor self-image in a junior high adolescent is merely an underdeveloped self-image that will mature naturally through normal experiences.

We can, however, give our children a double, confusing sense of self. Becky's dad praised her for being outspoken and independent. Becky's mom criticized her for these very same qualities because they seemed unfeminine and contrary to the mom's own self-image. Parents need to be consistent and work together in communicating acceptance and unconditional love to their children.

Exploring Scripture

In Romans 8:35 Paul asks us, "Who shall separate us from the love of Christ? Shall tribulation, or distress, or persecution, or famine, or nakedness, or peril, or sword?"

- How might we apply this list to our situation in life?

Paul answers this question in verses 38–39. "For I am persuaded that neither death nor life, nor angels nor principalities nor powers, nor things present nor things to come, nor height nor depth, nor any other created thing, shall be able to separate us from the love of God which is in Christ Jesus our Lord."

Taking Action

- Tell your children the stories of their births regularly. Birthdays are a great opportunity to remind them that they are precious to you. Play word games like "You know what I love about you?"

- Linger around the dinner table and have each of your children share what they like most about one other person at the table—no negatives allowed. How fun it is to have children who may have been quarreling earlier hear great things about themselves from their siblings!

- You and your children can keep a Success List of the victories and good qualities they've demonstrated in their lives. Record specific times when they have felt the loving help of the Lord.

#18 Tackling Money Attitudes

Check your goals as a dad and husband. Is your primary goal is to make your family happy or is your primary goal is to make your family holy?

Unfortunately, "happy" is often viewed as materially happy, and marriages and families fall apart as dads try to supply everyone's wish list of goods and gadgets. Too many men sacrifice themselves and ultimately their families on the altar of work and financial security.

For many, the greater sacrifice would be spending more time at home. I've heard dads lament over a delinquent son, "Where did I do wrong? I broke my back to give my kid everything he wanted." Or regarding the response of the husband whose wife who files for divorce, "Sure I put in a long day. What does she expect? She likes to spend it, doesn't she?"

The fact is for many men work is like an athletic competition. They thrive on the challenge of scoring sales, landing accounts, outsmarting the opponent. And money is the scorecard that depicts victory or loss. Tim was driven to reach the top in his real estate firm. He settled his family in a nice home in suburbia and felt like he'd given them half the world, although he was seldom home with them except to sleep. Certainly their lifestyle was far better than his when he was growing up. Tim often reminded his wife he'd take time for his kids when they were older and appreciated his attention more.

Once Tim's son and daughter hit junior high, however, they wanted nothing to do with Tim because he'd never established a relationship with them. In high school his older son actually resented it when Tim came to his basketball games.

Some husbands want their wives to work because they insist upon, but don't absolutely need, more money to get ahead. Although some families can't survive without two incomes, many can. Often wives long to stay home and meet the needs of their husbands and families as a creative homemaker, even if they must live on a limited budget.

The surprising frequency with which the topic of money appears in Scripture tells us money is an issue that cannot be ignored in training children. Certainly money is necessary, and money flows from work. Although most money questions from parents in counseling focus on a child's allowance, payment for household chores, and the like, the greatest challenge is teaching children a right attitude toward money.

It is critically important to avoid two dangerous attitudes about money:

1. Fear of not having enough money to buy what one needs to feel adequate (which stems from feelings of unworthiness and the false belief that material possessions will make you more special).

2. Overspending due to a constant hunger for more stuff (which stems from greed).

Some men love the thrill of business success and feel a sense of conquest through their work. Is this true of you?

Exploring Scripture

First Timothy 6:10 reads, "For the love of money is a root of all kinds of evil, for which some have strayed from the faith in their greediness, and pierced themselves through with many sorrows."

- How is money itself very helpful in life?

- How does the love of money get us into trouble?

Proverbs 8:18 says, "Riches and honor are with me, enduring riches and righteousness."

- What is the source of true, enduring riches and honor?

- Why is it so dangerous to be greedy?

Taking Action

Without inner feelings of self-worth, children read the reflections of themselves in the opinions of others. Sadly, even kids often measure worth by the possessions they can see.

- When have you judged others by their appearance or possessions?

- What experiences from your own life contributed to falling into this trap?

- Share with your children how this occurred. List some of the reasons why it's wrong.

- Write down ideas on how to avoid assessing a person's worth by material possessions. What should we focus on?

#19 Resisting Greed

Greed can take various subtle forms. When you are possessed by greed, it's impossible to pursue the holy life God has for you—a life of being a man in command under God to lead your family. Greed can take the form of the compulsive need to always get the best deal or the drive to always come out on top. Greed involves the deception that there's something that can be bought that will care for you and meet your needs in a way you cannot, Christ cannot, and another person cannot. The seeds of greed are often sown in childhood. Fears of financial insufficiency established in childhood can lead to greed. Do you have fears about money and possessions that are a carryover from your past?

Excessive bargain hunting is widespread today. The number of sales and flea markets readily attests to this fact. The constant search for a bargain, however, is always not the virtue it may seem. Mark described how he used to feel a surge of adrenaline as he'd approach a home improvement outlet. "I'd buy more stuff I didn't need because it was such a deal. I'd tell myself I'd figure out what to do with it later. For instance I'd buy tools on sale. I raised a son with this same tendency. I've since learned to buy less and shop with greater care and less intensity."

You have a great, generous God who delights in giving to those who love Him. Be a wise steward of what He gives. The constant seeking of your own advantage is not prudence, but greed.

On the other side of the coin, repeatedly telling children you'll never be able to afford something can also plant in them an inordinate desire for wealth. Financial positions can change for better or for worse. Continually harping at the kids about turning the lights off because you won't be able to pay the bill and saying things like "I don't know where the money will come from" can create insecurity. It gives children an unhealthy, obsessive focus on money. Such messages create a fear that can lead to covetousness. Your children's source of security becomes money instead of God. Teach your children to trust Christ. He will meet their needs.

Exploring Scripture

As the Israelites traveled through the wilderness, God gave them everything they needed. Exodus 12:38 reads, "A mixed multitude went up with them also, and flocks and herds—a great deal of livestock." Deuteronomy 2:6–7 tells us, "You shall buy food from them [the descendants of Esau] with money, that you may eat; and you shall also buy water from them with money, that you may drink." They brought money and livestock from Egypt that God had provided for their journey.

- Have there been times when you felt God did not know of your needs?

Taking Action

- List a time with your family when God has supplied your needs.

- Ask others in the family to share times they've wanted something and how God has taken care of their desires and needs.

#20 Handling Finances Carefully

The healthy balanced perspective on money is you work for it and God gives it to you. You can get into trouble when you start thinking you get it by your own efforts—that your work rather than God's provision is where money comes from. First Timothy 6:9–10 warns against loving money.

Loving money is sinful because it leads to loving self, prestige, security, and material things more than loving God. You should be in control of money rather than money being in control of you. Handling money properly is tougher today than ever before in history. Through TV, radio, and magazines, you're continually bombarded by tempting advertising purposely aimed at creating new desires within you. Both the body and brain can get you in big trouble by always being hungry for more of anything that looks good.

Jim had a successful business, a summer home, a big boat, snowmobiles, and lots of friends (of course). He worked hard and partied hard. One of those friends stole the heart of his wife, and she asked Jim for a divorce. Suddenly, he stopped playing with all his toys and realized how devastated he'd be without his wife and children. Only when he started trusting Jesus did he manage to win her back. They still have all those material things, but they don't get in the way of his attending church every week and working to be an attentive husband and father.

Jesus' personal example gives us many clear pictures of how to live in this world with the right attitude toward money. Jesus, who always lived in complete submission to His Father, was neither physically nor spiritually poor. Jesus had plenty of food. Jesus worked with the disciples, He taught the multitudes, He healed the sick. He was a welcome guest in many homes and treated with generous hospitality.

Rather than watching the balance in a checkbook, Jesus kept reinvesting His spiritual wealth. He didn't "spend more" than He had. Jesus started His earthly ministry "prayed up" during His forty days in the wilderness, but He didn't miss His solitary time with the Father every day, no matter how many people clamored for His attention. When necessary, He sent the people away. Focusing on our spiritual accounts will keep both our relationships and our finances in proper balance.

Exploring Scripture

There's nothing wrong with being rich. The Bible tells us in Genesis 13:2 that "Abram was very rich in livestock, in silver, and in gold." Some Christians look disdainfully at other Christians who are well off—a form of reverse snobbery.

Then again, there's no guilt in being poor. James 2:5 says, "Listen, my beloved brethren: Has God not chosen the poor of this world to be rich in faith and heirs of the kingdom which He promised to those who love Him?" Your children need to understand that being poor isn't a reason for thinking less of anyone.

The very real danger is that sin enters into riches when we begin to trust in wealth. "Because you say, 'I am rich, have become wealthy, and have need of nothing'—and do not know that you are wretched, miserable, poor, blind, and naked—" (Revelation 3:17).

Taking Action

Jesus knew we'd always have the physically or spiritually poor here on earth—some because of their own unwillingness to follow the principles in God's Word and some because of the sin of those around them.

Because of greed, some people sinfully take advantage of others—they do not pay just wages, they lie, cheat, or steal. Because of laziness, some people refuse to work.

- Can you think of some warning signs in your own family that money is taking too prominent a position?

#21 Increasing Self-Control

Self-control is mastery over your body through wise decisions and behavior in every area of your life. Self-control helps you keep your promises to God and to your family, keeps the things heaped into your life from burying you alive and choking off your critical supply line to Jesus and other people.

Self-control is usually developed over time. It requires learning the meaning of enough and curbing excessive fleshly desires. Fasting periodically can help you gain mastery over your body. You may think fasting involves becoming gaunt from lack of food. Far from it. Fasting can be skipping lunch or desserts for a week or giving up something you enjoy like cola drinks. The point is exercising control and discipline by limiting yourself, particularly in a sensual area. Isaiah 58:3–14 describes methods and benefits of fasting. He suggests it includes giving bread to the poor and trying to help those who are treated unjustly. Fasting can also be refraining from gossip, and refusing to point your finger at others and speak maliciously or boastfully.

The importance of sacrificially limiting yourself is often downplayed in our present pleasure-loving society. Fasting helps you control your bodily desires and emotional impulses. Then, when you need to say no to a material temptation, you know you've power over your body because you've practiced the discipline of self-control. This transfers to all areas of your life like using self-control in regard to spending—even occasionally doing without something nice, but not essential that you'd like to buy.

Refusing to get involved in work or strenuous recreation on the Lord's Day is also a method of using self-control to please God. God's Word tells us to honor the Sabbath, call it a delight, and turn from doing as you please on God's holy day (Isa. 58:13). A weekly Sabbath day is God's gift to give you a real opportunity to recharge. Take advantage of the rest He wants you to have. Experience the benefits of weekly worship and renewal.

Exploring Scripture

Second Peter 1:5–8 says, "But also for this very reason, giving all diligence, add to your faith virtue, to virtue knowledge, to knowledge self-control, to self-control perseverance, to perseverance godliness, to godliness brotherly kindness, and to brotherly kindness love. For if these things are yours and abound, you will be neither barren nor unfruitful in the knowledge of our Lord Jesus Christ."

Isaiah 58:9 tells us, "Then you shall call and the Lord will answer; you shall cry and He will say, 'Here I am.'"

• Trace the path shown here from diligence in learning to practicing love.

• What do these verses say about the importance of self-discipline in spiritual growth.

Taking Action

• Name some specific ways you can increase self-control in your life.

• What practical steps might you take in order to practice fasting?

#22 Resisting Advertising Temptations

Advertisements are designed to demonstrate how helpful or essential a product is. In short, advertisement makes acquiring certain items seem like a must. You know that advertising appeals to your sense of self—to the ego, the desire for status, ease, and entertainment. Yet it works on you.

In our materialistic, media-saturated society, it's important that you help your children see through the messages communicated by advertisers. Studies over the past few years have shown that children as young as three and four readily recognize commercial characters such as Joe Camel or the now retired beer dog, Spud McKenzie. How amazing is that!

Advertising often plays upon human insecurity- the natural tendency of many adults and adolescents to feel as if they don't measure up to some invisible standard of worth or beauty. Commercials say you're inadequate without certain things and that you will feel good about yourself only if you own something you don't already have. Insecurity and fear can push you into making foolish purchasing decisions.

Greed says enough is not enough; only by having more than you need will you be able to feel secure.

If you don't see yourself as an OK person just as you are, it's easy to be swayed into believing that some external thing will make you better. Remember your identity is in Christ and what He says about you. His Word says you're complete in Him!

Teach your children that even if they had all the money they wanted and could buy whatever they liked, they'd find that things alone don't make them happy. What's the benefit of being prideful by showing off that you've got the best? Being the envy of others is only a brief thrill and often, ironically, drives others away.

Exploring Scripture

Paul wrote in Philippians 4:11, "Not that I speak in regard to need, for I have learned in whatever state I am, to be content."

Resisting advertising's temptations is not accomplished overnight. Notice that Paul says he has learned to be content. Before we can teach our children what true contentment is, we need to learn to be content ourselves.

- In what ways have you experienced a sense of discontent?

- Have you dealt with those feelings in a positive or negative manner.

Taking Action

- What items are you most often tempted to overspend on?

- What was the last thing you bought that you didn't really need?

- What are you considering buying that you could do without?

- What better use might you put that money toward?

#23 Answering Money Questions

Dad, here are some questions to ask yourself about money.

1. Are you living within your income?

2. Are you being too tight with spending your money on your family's needs and some of their wants, too?

3. What do you really need to make you happy?

4. If you can't afford something that you'd like to have, can you conclude it's obviously not part of God's plan that you should have it now?

5. Can anyone wear two coats or two pairs of shoes at once? How would you explain this concept to your children?

6. What changes do you need to make in your purchasing habits?

7. Is your generosity toward your wife and children a reflection of God's generosity?

One way to take control of your money is to be a generous giver. Let your children see you clean your closet and pack up some of your better clothes to give to the needy, not just your discards.

Give tangible gifts that are not tax deductible as well as cash or checks. Whenever possible give anonymously. For example, send gift certificates by mail to people who need encouragement.

We made a commitment never to pass an offering basket without giving something. Even if the cause isn't extremely important, the action of giving molds the spirit of generosity in us.

Should you give to panhandlers? Giving cash alone may be a waste if the panhandler is on alcohol or other drugs. It's best to buy a meal or some specific item they need. If you choose to give a gift, along with your gift tell the person that money is important, but what's most important is free—the love of God in Christ Jesus. Explain how you or any Bible-believing church will help them know more about Jesus. Encourage them to read God's Word.

Exploring Scripture

In 1 Thessalonians 5:21 we read, "Test all things; hold fast what is good." It's always a good practice to test yourself and your attitudes periodically. It helps keep you on track, working toward your goals, and keeping your promises.

- What or who has most influenced your own view of money and material things?

- What negatives do you need to reject and what positives do you need to hold on to?

Taking Action

- Look back over the questions and your answers above, and select one change you can implement right now.

- Sit down and make a list with your family of ways you could demonstrate generosity to someone.

#24 Making A Family History

Just as individual nations and races have a particular history, so too does a family. Each has a peculiar character as well. Some are highly organized units, some more spontaneous and casual. Some families have strong verbal communication systems. Others tend more toward action. All have their stories from the past to tell. How far back can you trace your family's history?

You develop a family history as you help nurture the unique personality of each of your children. Pinpointing and discussing family history can be a source of pride and satisfaction to children. This is what Jewish families did as they passed down the stories of Jewish ancestors like Noah, Abraham and Sarah, Daniel, Ruth, and David.

As you share the stories about the people in your family line with your children, look for any traits that seem to be a family pattern. Have members of your family been attracted to specific

Occupations like teaching, mechanical trades, the military, law? How did grandparents and great-grandparents meet? Has there been a hero in the family who has done something particularly courageous? Write down these stories and tell them orally to your children as well.

Even more important, what are some of the interesting stories from your childhood or your courtship? Have you had a chance to be a hero? When have you stuck your neck out as a Christian, taken an unpopular stand at work, or participated in a Christian protest? What made you choose your career? Write down some of your own stories and tell your children about the circumstances that have shaped your life. You'll become a real-life role model to them.

Periodically praise your wife's and children's accomplishments in front of your other family members as well as outsiders. Tell positive stories about them that others will learn and repeat in the future.

Does one member of your family seem to be the point of jokes, the one blamed for problems more than any other? Whether deserved or not, this can be hurtful. Avoid having a family scapegoat—one person everyone dumps on who becomes the heavy for the family. This unfair partiality creates a destructive family history for everyone involved. It enables family members to avoid facing up to their own inadequacies by always focusing on the inadequacies of someone else in the family.

Giving your children historical continuity helps to expand their small worlds. They should know that all of life does not revolve around them. A family history provides children with the larger perspective that they are a part of something much bigger than their everyday experience.

Exploring Scripture

The Bible records God's great love for His people and His desire that they not forget past lessons of faith. God commanded Israel in Deuteronomy 6:6–9, 12 as follows:

And these words which I command you today shall be in your heart. You shall teach them diligently to your children, and shall talk of them when you sit in your house, when you walk by the way, when you lie down, and when you rise up. You shall bind them as a sign on your hand, and they shall be as frontlets between your eyes. You shall write them on the doorposts of your house and on your gates. . . . then beware lest you forget the LORD who brought you out of the land of Egypt, from the house of bondage.

- What benefits would obeying this command bring to Israel? Do the same with your family history and your spiritual history to learn from the mistakes of the past and to strengthen your positive qualities.

Taking Action

- On a large piece of paper draw a family tree with many branches. Write the names of your family members as far back as you know.

- Begin to collect and write down stories from your family heritage as far back as possible.

- Write down stories from your own life, especially your spiritual story of conversion.

- Begin writing stories from the lives of your children—give them a recorded history, too!

#25 Learning to Lighten Up

Learning to lighten up is an important, and often neglected lesson you can teach your children. Pushing and trying too hard can sabotage your children's efforts. This phenomenon is best explained in terms of athletics. Athletes who are favored to win an event sometimes perform poorly. Others, with less to lose but who are out to do their best no matter what, often perform better.

When little outside pressure is exerted but children feel confident that they can do well, they seem to do their best. Giving too much attention to the outcome of performance can hinder natural ability. Children should focus on enjoying the process of performance more than being concerned about the outcome. For example, Wayne remembers talking to our daughter, Pam, about a big basketball game she had coming up, supposedly a must-win games. By talking frequently about how she would have to play her best, etc. Wayne made Pam very tense. By game time she was not herself and did not play her usual great game. He learned an important lesson.

Public speaking is another area where too much focus on performance hinders the natural process. It's best to focus on the content of the speech rather than on exactly how it's going to be delivered. The area of social performance causes great pressure for adolescents, particularly in making small talk and asking for dates.

The combination of pressure to perform well and an underdeveloped self-image often botch what your child could do naturally. Both intensify the fear of failure. It's true children need discipline and determination to achieve realistic goals, but children also need to relax and not fear failure.

Exploring Scripture

Read what Paul tells us about perfection in Philippians 3:12— "Not that I have already attained, or am already perfected; but I press on, that I may lay hold of that for which Christ Jesus has also laid hold of me."

- How did Paul's focus affect his view of himself and the future?

Taking Action

Teach your children to:

- be wise risk-takers

- expect some failure—it's inevitable

Remind your children often that:

- failure can be positive

- very failure may contain a seed of future success.

- What examples from your own life illustrate these statements?

- List the strengths and weaknesses you've already noticed in your children.

- Pray about how you can you encourage them without adding extra pressure.

Here are words you might use: "I'm proud of you for trying." "I don't expect you to excel at everything; nobody does."

- Write down others encouraging phrases you can think of.

#26 Coping with Perfectionism

Performance and self-worth are not measured equally, but often get lumped together. Christ gives us a sense of self-esteem that has nothing to do with performance or personal effort. Teaching your children the difference between these concepts increases their self-understanding and enables them to gear down an excessive desire for praise from other people. It's tough to admit but the real reason individuals like to achieve perfection is usually to receive the praise of others. Ask your children if they're trying to please you, other people, or God. Evaluate yourself as well. How about your own attitudes about perfection?

You'll never succeed if you set yourself up to please others. People are too fickle. You can be a hero one day and fall out of favor with people the next day. On the other hand God delights in all your efforts. And He doesn't expect perfection. That's reserved for heavenly surroundings. Why ask more of yourself or your children than God requires of you?

It's wise to remember that a child who can't exhibit "perfect" behavior in a situation, like keeping his or her room neat or performing well in school, may give up trying altogether. That's far less frustrating to a youngster. It's not that they don't care. Some children are obsessive-compulsive; they care and want to please too much and can't stand to fail. These children need to become comfortable with a realistic, more relaxed standard and learn to enjoy doing things for their own inherent satisfaction.

Exploring Scripture

The Pharisees attempted to perfectly observe every dot of the law, and they expected others to do the same. No one could achieve their standard of perfection. Loving approval sets a person up for constant pressure to perform at a level no one could achieve and consistently maintain.

John 12:42–43 reads, "Nevertheless even among the rulers many believed in Him [Jesus], but because of the Pharisees they did not confess Him, lest they should be put out of the synagogue; for they loved the praise of men more than the praise of God."

• How did the Pharisees' perfectionism affect the lives of others?

• How can a person's perfectionistic drives undermine his walk with Christ?

Taking Action

• Are there any perfectionistic standards you have for yourself that you need to relax?

• Are there any perfectionistic standards you have for your spouse that you need to relax?

• Are there perfectionistic standards you have for your children that you need to relax?

• Have you noticed a tendency to perfectionism in your children that you can help them deal with? What are they?

- Write down statements you can use to reinforce a more realistic standard of performance in your children. Practice saying them aloud.

#27 Relieving Performance Pressure

Our children, from birth to preschool and through the awkward years of adolescence, are not "miniature" adults. It seems an obvious concept, but it's one that adults often quickly forget. Kids are just that—kids. They will do some things that are childish and less than perfect, if not downright dumb or stupid from an adult's perspective. But more importantly, children want to do well, want to please their parents, and want acceptance and admiration from their peers. Those expectations can place considerable pressure on their development.

Children are not going to be perfect nor are they always going to do well. When they are disappointed with themselves (or sense that you are disappointed with them), they may say things like "I'm so stupid!" or "I'm just no good at this!" Remind your children that they can do better in the future if they don't do well at first. Sure, they probably know they can improve in the future, but it's easy to forget and become discouraged in the crushing times of disappointment.

Tell your children they won't always perform up to par and that's okay. No adults do either. Refuse to beat yourself or them over the head when they don't perform well. Isn't this one of the most important lessons of maturity? Lyn, a highly motivated young person we know, who was All-Star in basketball. Her dad had to assure her it was okay not to be MVP each game.

Remember excessive praise can hamper performance when it adds more pressure to succeed. Stan's mom and dad raised him with constant demands for high performance. Poor Stan is so determined to measure up to his parents' standard of excellence that he functions in a high-speed frenzy. He's demanding and pushy with others and has become his own worst enemy. His driven personality turns off both his colleagues and his superiors at work. Recently let go from his fourth corporate job, Stan is still yearning to measure up to his mom's and dad's demands for achievement.

Exploring Scripture

"As a father pities his children, so the LORD pities [has compassion for] those who fear Him. For He knows our frame; He remembers that we are dust" (Psalm 103:13–14).

• Why does God have compassion for us, His children?

• How can we earthly fathers copy our heavenly Father as we instruct our children?

Taking Action

• Do you remember a time in your life when you faced performance pressure?

• How did you handle it?

• Is your child experiencing performance pressure in any area right now? In what area(s)?

• What lessons can you teach your children from your experience?

#28 Dealing With Deadlines

When making any decision that involves a big change, people may postpone deciding until time has closed the door on some of their choices. They're so concerned about making the right decision that they "freeze up." Often this means they end up with even fewer options. An honor student and outstanding athlete we know waited so long to pick a college that only one school was still available.

Very few adults, young people, or children really do best under time pressure despite their claims to the contrary. Therefore, it's easy to jump to the false conclusion that deadlines are the problems. Here's an important distinction—pressure to perform well is not the same as having a deadline. People who say they do best under pressure often really mean they perform best with a realistic deadline. Children and adults who tend to procrastinate will not perform at all unless they must. The "must" is a consistent and realistic deadline and time schedule.

Is this an issue for you or your wife or kids? Do you model planning ahead? Sit down with your children regularly and ask what deadlines they're facing in their lives right now. How have they scheduled themselves to meet them? One of the most overlooked reasons children do poorly in school is because they don't know how to plan their assignment time realistically. Check out whether lack of confidence is the cause of procrastination.

It's up to Dad and Mom, too, to identify your child's strengths and limitations and help your children learn to meet deadlines, whether it's preparing for an athletic event, a piano recital, or a school project. Focus on how to achieve the desired goals in the time period allowed they need to practice? Discuss the level of performance desired in any activity. A good rule is: encourage competence but discourage perfectionism.

Exploring Scripture

Consider Genesis 1:31–2:2. "Then God saw everything that He had made, and indeed it was very good. So the evening and the morning were the sixth day. Thus the heavens and the earth, and all the host of them, were finished. And on the seventh day God ended His work which He had done, and He rested on the seventh day from all His work which He had done."

- How many days did it God take to create the world? Six days, not one. God might have pushed it all into one day but He chose to pace Himself. Shouldn't you do the same and teach your children to do the same?

For In-Depth Study

Read the first chapter of Genesis, noticing how God planned out His work over a period of time.

Taking Action

- What is the next project facing you or your child? Sit down and discuss the best way to complete it well without undue pressure. Make a plan with your child and check up on the work without nagging.

#29 Seeing the Good in Your Past

Charlie, a counseling client of mine (name changed), talked often about his childhood. "Until I was thirty-five, my parents were full-blown alcoholics. My mom, bless her heart, was non-functional, for all practical purposes. Sometimes we ate dinner at nine or ten, more often we didn't eat supper at all. Despite our upper-middle-class status, my sisters and I raided the cabinets for whatever food we could find. The house was cleaned when we kids did it or my dad hired a cleaning service."

"My dad endured by ignoring my mom and spending all his time either at work or at a cocktail lounge after work, supposedly involved in semi-business transactions for his construction company. Meanwhile, at home Mom was often passed out or in a drunken stupor on the sofa. She was kind and gentle on the surface, but inside she was a self-centered child who didn't want to deal with the realities of work or the monotony of home. Childhood excursions were nonexistent."

"Fun-type family interactions were zero. I never heard my mom express interest in spiritual matters, praise my school achievements, or ask me if I was happy. When I had a childhood illness, I was treated as an annoyance rather than a concern."

"The result?" Charlie said, "is me, an emotionally-starved child from an upper-middle-class home with a super drive to achieve. It was years later as an adult before I could separate who I was from what I did—a superb example of the worth-equals-performance syndrome." This is a common problem with children of alcoholics.

After several counseling sessions Charlie began to see that his childhood, as painful as it was at times, had produced some good qualities in him and taught him important principles. He said,

"All my life I loved my parents although I never wanted to imitate any part of their lifestyle. But I did learn to be independent and caring, and I later went into social work." He concluded, "Don't feel sorry for me. Beneath the self-centeredness and hurt my parents inflicted on my sisters and me, I knew I was loved even though it was a performance-based love. And I knew I was needed by my family. I'd learned as a little child that God was my best buddy. Even as a preschool child, I talked with Him constantly in my loneliness. I knew God was real."

Perhaps your childhood wasn't as extreme and painful as Charlie's, but every family is dysfunctional in some areas to one degree or another. There's no such thing as a perfect human family. Every family has its strengths and weaknesses. You learn many of your most valuable lessons for the rest of life through the difficult times of your childhood. These are some of the treasures from your past that you can now teach your children.

Exploring Scripture

Hebrews 12:2 reminds us, "Looking unto Jesus, the author and finisher of our faith, who for the joy that was set before Him endured the cross, despising the shame, and has sat down at the right hand of the throne of God."

- Does the Lord's example help us in looking back over the difficult times of our own lives?

For In-Depth Study

Read over the story of Joseph meeting his brothers in Genesis 45:1–15.

- Are there situations in your own life where broken relationships can be healed because of what God has done in your life?

Taking Action

- What difficult situations do you recall from your childhood?
- What helpful principles did your childhood teach you?
- What's your earliest memory of sensing God's love is real and personal for you?

#30 Being Your Wife's Partner

Being a man in command and a good husband involves more than sexual faithfulness and putting food on the table. It also means helping your wife find fulfillment and joy in family life. Is your wife's work often ignored or is she involved in too much drudgery?

Good spouses not only know their tasks, but they know one another. They sense when one is tired and needs a break. They pitch in and carry a little more of the load. They stay focused on the goal of unity rather than looking for ways "do their own thing."

Observe whether your wife gets enough of her personal needs met. Take the kids for an outing with daddy to the park or perhaps to a baseball or football game so mom has some time for herself.

Does your wife need some adult company after a day of parenting preschoolers? Get the little ones to bed early and spend time together just talking or listening to music. Watching sports together on TV is probably not her first choice unless she's a sports fan! Maybe she just needs a quiet hour with you.

Being sensitive to your wife's needs requires commitment to make the task of parenting and running a household a shared responsibility. When you're home, are you really there or is your mind still at work? Do you see time spent at home as an infringement upon your personal time or an investment in the lives of your family that produces personal satisfaction? Wives need to know that their husbands are partners in marriage and parenting - really partners, not supervisors or part-timers.

Encourage your wife to have fun-filled interactions the children. Help her plan and carry out experiences with the children that go beyond the daily tasks of menu planning, grocery shopping, and providing transportation. I used to love playing soccer, basketball or tennis with my children. Without fun times the daily routine can become a mind numbing rut for moms caring for young children day in and day out.

Make family outings a regular part of the routine—on a weekly basis if at all possible. These events need not be expensive or exhausting and should be planned keeping the ages and interests of your children in mind. Younger children will probably not enjoy an all-day trip to a flea market. Older children will hold up longer! Younger children will look forward to trips to the park, visits to the zoo, shopping for pumpkins in the fall, or playing at the beach.

Older children may enjoy more active adventures such as a hike in the woods, miniature golf, skating, sightseeing trips, or visits to museums.

Exploring Scripture

Proverbs 31:10–11 says, "Who can find a virtuous wife? For her worth is far above rubies. The heart of her husband safely trusts her; so he will have no lack of gain."

- Do you truly value your wife? What are the "gains" she has brought you as a person?

And Ephesians 5:28 says, "So husbands ought to love their own wives as their own bodies; he who loves his wife loves himself."

- Everything you want to achieve in your relationships with your children you also want your wife to achieve with them.

- What principle does this verse give you to achieve that goal?

Taking Action

- Write down all the roles your wife plays in your household (cook, disciplinarian, etc.).

- How does her list of roles compare with your own?

- What can you do to encourage a more personal, fun-based relationship between your wife and your children?

- How can you help your wife fulfill some of her unmet goals?

#31 Developing Dependence

You've heard that's it's important to develop independence in our children. Developing dependence is also desirable. Schools, television, and magazines bombard children and young people with the message that they have the answer to any dilemma. The concepts of dependency and codependency nowadays are often viewed as distasteful and harmful. Who would suggest that dads and moms teach dependence?

The major question, however, is not dependence. All of us are dependent upon others to one degree or another. The real issue is dependence on whom and what?

Dads, help your sons and daughters realize that it's good to be dependent on God first of all and secondly on you and your wife. You're to be sources of emotional support throughout their lives. Teach your children to have confidence in our all-powerful God. How do you get this message of dependence and confidence in God across to your children?

Like every important spiritual lesson in life, this one is easier said than done. First of all, you'll need to be honest. Do you depend mostly on God or on yourself? Does your child see that you're willing to depend on God no matter what? Your example is the best teacher.

Can you have confidence in God when you're told your child has only hours to live? Can you depend on God when you have a mortgage payment due and no steady income? We must intellectually and emotionally grasp God's sovereign love, and we must trust His ways in such moments.

Dependence and confidence is like that tiny, yet mighty mustard seed you've heard about in the Bible. It's the tiniest of seeds in Palestine, yet it grows to be the largest shrub in the Middle East reaching tree-size at maturity. Jesus compared faith to a mustard seed. A little dependence and trust begins the growth process. Continued dependence and trust slowly nurture a strong confidence in the Lord and growth as a believer.

Exploring Scripture

Psalm 118:8–9 reads, "It is better to trust in the LORD than to put confidence in man. It is better to trust in the LORD than to put confidence in princes."

- We depend on and have confidence in various sorts of things. Think about some of the things you trust in.

Taking Action

- When were you most recently dependent upon another person to do something for you? How did it turn out?

- When were you last aware of being completely dependent upon God to work on your behalf?

#32 Trusting

In what area of great importance in your life right now do you totally need to trust God? How about in your child's life? Maybe it's doing well on school assignments or tests. Maybe your daughter is trying to make the girls' basketball team or your son is trying to make new friends in the junior high class.

Perhaps these don't seem like a "big deal" to us, but for our kids these can assume life-and death proportion. Be aware of the concerns and struggles that your children are facing. Pray aloud for them before they leave to take that test or go to the team tryout. Show them your confidence in God is real and He's a present help for all of us.

The prayer we prayed often for our children during their school years was: "Lord, let them perform to the best of their ability, and then some. They've studied (or practiced). You know their knowledge and their capabilities; give them answers they didn't even know they knew (or let them play even better than they normally can) by Your grace and love. And Lord, we give You all the glory for the results." The sounds of our children scurrying out the door and—just before the slam - yelling "Don't forget to pray for me!" are precious memories.

It's fine to pray that they do their best, but also important to keep achievement in perspective—"for God's glory." Encourage your children to have a sense of humility when they do well. We ultimately owe the credit to Him for whatever we accomplish.

Your children will see that prayer has power. Your home will be your children's first prayer laboratory. They'll learn that you believe strongly that God is a miracle-working God. They can relax because whatever happened had been committed to God.

If our children, Pam or Dan or David or Tamara, played great at a sports event or did well on a test, we all rejoiced. If not, despite the fact that he or she had prepared well, then God had a reason, and it was not to punish or disappoint.

Perhaps someone else on the other team needed this victory more than they did. Maybe God has a better activity or sport for the use of their time. Or maybe they slacked off in their responsibility to study and prepare for the test. In this nonthreatening framework, you can openly discuss the consequences—whatever they are.

Remember to pray for your own needs, too, and share the answered prayers with your children. This is how you can model your trust in our heavenly Father.

Exploring Scripture

Notice what Jeremiah 17:7–8 says:

"Blessed is the man who trusts in the LORD,
And whose hope is the LORD.
For he shall be like a tree planted by the waters,
Which spreads out its roots by the river,
And will not fear when heat comes;
But its leaf will be green,
And will not be anxious in the year of drought,

Nor will cease from yielding fruit."
What are some lessons in trust this passage tells us?

Taking Action

- What's your child trusting God for right now?

- What are you trusting God for right now?

#33 Getting Involved

Your impact on the lives of your growing children is one of the most powerful formative influences they'll ever have. It's the trendy thing for dads to be involved in caring for babies. The problem is that once past the "I'll help out with diapers and hauling the baby paraphernalia" period, dads sometimes don't know how to translate this desire to be involved into action at the next stage.

A man can be home every night but be emotionally distant from the people he loves the most. Why are some men reluctant to be emotionally involved in the lives of their children?

Perhaps it's a carryover from growing up in a home where dad was the silent figure behind the newspaper every evening—present but about as lively as a potted plant!

Perhaps not wanting to get involved in your family life is a matter of stress. The pressures of work and the hours required just to put food on the table leave you too mentally exhausted to concentrate on the concerns of young children.

Or something more common may be at work in your thinking. You may feel that being involved in the pretend games, the scraped knees, the bedtime stories, and all the time and energy-consuming parts of childrearing just isn't "your thing." What you really mean is that these activities don't naturally appeal, which means you're replacing your own self-interest above the emotional needs of your children.

A lack of engagement in the day-to-day life of your children carries with it tremendous danger. Emotional distancing can be interpreted by children as a lack of worth on their part. If you or their mom doesn't seem to care deeply about them, it must somehow be their fault they assume. They may try to somehow earn daddy's attention by being perfect (a hopeless task adults know) or by acting up (which at least produces negative attention from dad).

Dads do you have a daily routine that provides time for your children to feel a physical and emotional bond with you? Do younger children look forward to a hug or a short wrestle with you when you come in the door? Can older children count on you to greet them and ask what happened during their day even if they look like talking is the last thing on their minds! Do they know that every night they can count on you to tuck them in or sit on the edge of their bed to discuss a problem?

Getting involved may is no more difficult than the principle that Nike made famous:

"Just do it."

Exploring Scripture

"For God so loved the world that He gave His only begotten Son, that whoever believes in Him should not perish but have everlasting life." Also consider John 10:10: "I have come that they may have life, and that they may have it more abundantly" (John 3:16).

- To what extent was God willing to become involved with each of us?

Taking Action

- How much of your time on a weekly basis is really available to your family?

- What priorities do you need to change in your present schedule to make more time for your family?

#34 Going Fishing

What kind of memories are you creating in your child? Do you and your child regularly have fun one-on-one? Wayne is a spectator sports aficionado, something less than a fanatic but certainly more than casual fan. Our son David is less so. It amazed Wayne that not all our children shared his intense interest in sports. Wayne had to search to find a special dad-son activity he and David could share and fishing was it.

Recently, I was sitting at sunset on the deck of our Wisconsin lakefront home. Our son Dave was fishing alone on the pier as shadows stretched across the purple and orange sky. The next day Dave and his new bride would leave for graduate school in Virginia, and that night I could see the nostalgia in his faraway gaze as he said a silent good-bye to us and to his place of refuge. Here he and Wayne had spent hours whirling nylon lines and hearing the gentle plopping sound of little waves against the shore. Weighty matters had been shared while they fished together. How great these moments were for both of them! An incredible bonding took place that will last a lifetime.

Dads, experiment to discover what sport or recreation you can share with your child. The search is worthwhile. Maybe your child's a computer buff, but you're ignorant or bored by technology. Let him or her teach you, Dad. You can be a willing learner to spend time with your child.

God has His own reasons for your children's different interests. These attractions to various activities are part of the way He moves your children to fulfill the unique plan He has for each of their lives. Be sensitive to their interests and inclinations and help develop them even as you use their interests as a natural setting for your interactions with them.

As you share a leisure-time activity with each child, you can model and teach coping skills.

You'll demonstrate how to deal with moments of frustration as well as moments of success. This is the setting in which your private jokes develop and gentle banter can flow. These private times together are your brief opportunities for shaping your child's life for years to come.

Exploring Scripture

Deuteronomy 6:6–7 "And these words which I command you today shall be in your heart. You shall teach them diligently to your children, and shall talk of them when you sit in your house, when you walk by the way, when you lie down, and when you rise up."

- How does this directive for father-child interaction differ from our usual concept of what "teaching" means?

For In-Depth Study

Read the book of Proverbs with your child and discuss what you read. There are thirty-one chapters, read one chapter a day for a month. Or take it in smaller sections, perhaps a verse or two a day.

You and your child will be amazed at how Solomon's advice sounds like it was written for today.

Taking Action

- Write the name of each of your children and/or grandchildren here and list a possible activity the two of you might enjoy.

#35 Knowing Abba Father

Abba is like our word "daddy." Abba or "Father" is a term of endearment for God. How many children know God with deep love as Abba?

As a Christian counselor, I always probe my clients' concept of God. I want to know if they believe that God cares intensely and personally about what happens to them and that He chooses to be actively involved in their lives. Do they believe God has the power and desire to help them with problems? Or do they view God as some austere general checking troop movements from some distant part of the solar system?

A man's concept of his earthly father is one of the strongest influences on ideas of the fatherhood of God and the man's worth as a person. Over and over I observed clients assess their feelings for and impressions of their earthly fathers and then connect them to God.

Wow! Does this connection give you an incredible feeling of importance, Dad? It should.

You are an ambassador of God in the literal sense of the word. If you fail in the spiritual responsibilities of fathering, it may take years of retraining for your child to develop a correct understanding of the fatherhood of God.

Some men tend to think they must show either the harsher side of God through rigid discipline or the merciful side of God through disregard of any bad behavior. Neither approach shows Abba-style love to children.

For example, before Jed became a Christian, he admits his discipline with his three children was too harsh. But after he became a Christian, he quit disciplining his children entirely. He depended on his wife to do all the disciplining in their home. When he was alone with the children, he overlooked behavior that should have been corrected. That's not love; it's neglect. He finally learned to discipline appropriately without anger.

Dads, make sure your children understand these three things:

1. You want them to have fun and enjoy life.

2. You will discipline, admonish, exhort, and encourage them in love.

3. You will never stop loving them no matter how bad their behavior becomes.

These three things are true of the way the heavenly Father loves us. When you practice these principles, it's far easier for your children to have a healthy view of God.

Exploring Scripture

God gives you permission to have fun with your family! He even encourages spending some money for enjoyment and not just for necessities (see Deuteronomy 14:26). That means there can be a recreation category in your budget!

In fact, God commands His people to rejoice. Psalm 118:24 says, "This is the day the LORD has made; we will rejoice and be glad in it."

And He says He will never leave or forsake you or your children. Our heavenly Father makes this promise in both the Old and the New Testaments (see Genesis 28:15; Deuteronomy 31:6, 8; Joshua 1:5; Hebrews 13:5).

Taking Action

- What kind of Father is God? What adjectives would you use to describe Him?

- What kind of Father are you? What adjectives would you use to describe yourself?

- What changes do you need to make in your fathering to demonstrate Abba or "Daddy" love to your children?

#36 Developing Leadership

Leadership is willingness to take action, to do what needs doing combined with charismatic qualities of character. Godly leadership not only requires the right thoughts and feelings but also demands action, as Jesus so clearly demonstrated throughout His life.

A Mr. Nice-Guy-Who-Goes-with-the-Flow is rarely respected like a man who speaks with conviction and takes action when action is called for. The real leader isn't the one who yells the loudest; a strong leader can speak quietly but firmly and others will respond.

Don, a Christian man was wrestling with these issues. He admits he's reluctant to take a stand as a leader particularly among his friends. "I've got to push myself to take a position. It helps me to keep the example of Jesus in front of me."

Why are we reluctant to take the lead when discussing an issue or confronting a problem? For some men, personality factors are a factor. They're more laid back than others, less inclined to move into the spotlight and more comfortable in the background than the forefront.

For some, the simple fear of speaking to others in a group setting seems to paralyze their vocal cords. For still others, they feel that they simply don't know enough and will appear uninformed if they speak out.

No matter what your natural inclinations or inner fears, you can develop a greater sense of leadership and self-confidence by keeping a few basic principles in mind. As a believer, your authority flows from the truth of God's Word and the power of the Holy Spirit who is within you, helping you reach your goals. Your reliance upon the authority of God's Word should be evident to your children, your business associates, and your friends.

Don't shoot from the hip. If you haven't thought through an issue or considered all sides of a question (and there are rarely just two sides!), read what others have written, ask for opinions, and apply relevant Scripture passages to the situation.

Keep the right attitude when it comes to issues and to people. Debate an issue, but never degrade a person who disagrees with you. Even those who oppose with you will listen to your opinion when it's given with consideration and respect.

Exploring Scripture

Look at the examples of Jesus' style of leadership. In Matthew 13:36 "Jesus sent the multitude away and went into the house." When Jesus said go, people left. Jesus directed people in such a way that they listened and acted as He instructed.

Matthew 14:19–21 describes Jesus' feeding of five thousand people (with no advance call to the caterer). Jesus knew what He was going to do. He told the multitudes to sit down on the grass.

After the men, women, and children had been fed a free meal, they wanted to stick to Jesus like glue. Verse 22 says what happened next—"Immediately Jesus made ["Jesus strongly urged" as one commentator puts it] His disciples get into the boat and go before Him to the other side, while He sent the multitudes away."

Many of us might be tempted to keep that adoring crowd around, but Jesus knew that the Father's will involved more than just the popular opinion of others. As a leader, he took a course of action that others would have thought foolish, but He acted in complete confidence.

Matthew 12:38–39 says, "Then some of the scribes and Pharisees answered, saying, 'Teacher, we want to see a sign from You.' But He answered and said to them, 'An evil and adulterous generation seeks after a sign, and no sign will be given to it except the sign of the prophet Jonah.'"

When it was appropriate, Jesus said no to others. He was accountable to His Father before anyone else. "What would Jesus do?" is still one of the best questions you can ask yourself to direct your leadership.

Taking Action

- In what areas of your life - family relationships, work, or church fellowship do you need to become more of a leader and take charge?

#37 Becoming Holy

For a Christian, holiness is not an option; it's a priority. The word holy can be defined as follows:

- set apart to the service of God
- sacred
- characterized by perfection and transcendence

Perhaps you used to think holiness applied to priests, ministers, and elderly ladies who prayed all day and never associated the word with yourself. When Wayne read the Bible for the first time at age thirty-three, he was already the father of three children. He wanted to teach his daughters and his son to fish and golf and play basketball and be good students. It never occurred to him that he should model and teach holiness, whatever that was.

He now understands that being a Christian is more than a personal acknowledgment that Jesus is Lord. If you're under the headship of the Lord who has saved you from death, it's only natural that you desire to please Him and become like Him. That's holiness. Holiness requires having a clean and undivided heart before God.

You maintain a clean heart, of course, by monitoring your thought life. Are you being honest to confess our daily sins before the Lord and ask for His forgiveness and empowerment? Are you putting the light of God's Word on all the dark recesses of our fantasies and desires? Are you confessing your sins against others and seeking their forgiveness?

A holy heart has a singleness of purpose—it's not divided in its allegiance - on the one hand wanting to please God but on the other wanting to keep its options open. Being "set apart to the service of God" means that you belong to Him. If you allow a career or recreation or material thing to become a priority in your life, you're divided and no longer the exclusive property of the Lord.

The pressures and pleasures of this life can block your desire for holiness. The deception of wealth can lead you to think that holiness is less desirable than money. A heart filled with bitterness toward others can block your growth in holiness. Because these temptations are so prevalent, you need to be on guard to maintain your holiness. Acknowledge any sin immediately, confess it to God and to whoever else is involved, and ask for forgiveness.

Exploring Scripture

Leviticus 11:44 says, "For I am the LORD your God. You shall therefore consecrate yourselves, and you shall be holy; for I am holy."

• In what sense can God command us to be holy?

First Peter 1:16 says, "Because it is written, 'Be holy, for I am holy.'"

• Why is God's character the basis for our call to holiness?

Taking Action

You may wonder how you can grow in holiness. The answer is to immerse yourself in the ways of God as revealed in Scripture. Continually ask God to cleanse you from any contaminant.

- Spend time daily alone in the presence of God.

- What specific areas of your life need to be opened and made holy to God?

#38 Dealing with Offenders

When you forgive someone who's offended you and perhaps even do a kindness in return, you refuse to carry the load of having been wounded. It's like having a heart that instantly repairs itself. You have chosen the better way when you allow yourself to respond without envy or anger or bitterness.

Forgiveness can also act like shock therapy for the person you're forgiving. Abusers expect victims to strive to get even. They can't believe you'd be nice instead. You certainly confuse them—unless they have totally hardened consciences. However, helping your offender to change can't be your only motive for acting in forgiveness. Pleasing Jesus is your foremost goal.

Jesus Christ has high expectations for His followers. In Matthew 5:43–44 Jesus says, "You have heard that it was said, 'You shall love your neighbor and hate your enemy.' But I say to you, love your enemies, bless those who curse you, do good to those who hate you, and pray for those who spitefully use you and persecute you." What He asks us to do seems contrary to human nature, doesn't it?

It's not easy to respond to people in that way. Could Jesus really mean turn the other cheek and offer total forgiveness? And do good to your enemy? It's hard enough to truly forgive, let alone plan a way to do good to someone who has abused you! Maybe that's why Jesus gave the ultimate example from His cross.

There were times when Wayne would get angry with me or the children because of something we said or did that upset him. He had difficulty forgiving us immediately and dealing with his feelings of disappointment. His revenge consisted of not speaking to us for a while. (Maybe your revenge is yelling.) Wayne came to realize his behavior was wrong—definitely not what Jesus would do.

Carl built a new house on his own vacant lot next door to his neighbor. The neighbor became furious because he had gotten used to the unobstructed view of the woods, and there was no way the new house could be built without obstructing the neighbor's view. Was Carl in the wrong? No, of course not. He could build on his property. But the neighbor refused to speak to Carl or his family afterward and would turn his back and walk away if Carl approached him. To make sure Carl didn't develop bitterness toward his neighbor, Carl occasionally sent him anonymous gifts like candy or dinner certificates to a local restaurant.

Carl made this effort to avoid developing a bitter attitude toward his neighbor and it was an example of Christ's influence in his life. Wanting to be like Christ kept Carl pursuing holiness above all— even in the face of an undeserved grudge! Much mental illness and many wasted lives stem from the unwillingness to forgive others and protect ourselves from bitterness and anger.

Family relationships have been destroyed over who inherited the gun collection or the grandfather clock. It sounds ridiculous, but I've seen it happen. Satan loves it! Ironically, the one who offended you may not even have had control over the event. Forgiveness demonstrates to you as well as to your spouse and children who observe your behavior (more closely than you can imagine) that you're impenetrable at the core. And you are! That core within you is Christ.

He bore the hurt and rejection of the multitudes yet returned in resurrection power to offer salvation to the entire world.

Exploring Scripture

In regard to fighting for rights, we need to heed the instruction in 1 Corinthians 6:7. "Why do you not rather accept wrong? Why do you not rather let yourselves be defrauded?"

- What does it say about dealing with wrongs?

- Isn't that totally contrary to all this stick-up-for-your-rights talk?

The truth is, we should stick up for what we believe, not for our rights. The responsibility of fighting for our rights rests with God! Nehemiah 4:20 says, "Our God will fight for us." Exodus 14:14 says, "The LORD will fight for you, and you shall hold your peace."

- What risks do we take in following this principle?

Taking Action

Think of the enemies in your life at present or in the past.

- When have you failed to deal with an offender as Jesus would?

- What changes will you make to be more like Christ in this area?

- Jot down some things you could do (like Carl) for someone who wouldn't expect a kindness from you.

#39 Forgiving and Saying You're Sorry

The willingness to forgive others and the readiness to say you're sorry are essential ways for a man in command to exalt Christ. Forgiving others and saying you're sorry (sometimes even when you're not in the wrong) have nothing to do with allowing yourself to be pushed around.

Christ does not advocate continuing in situations where others can take advantage of you. Only once, when He chose to undergo rejection and crucifixion for the greater good of saving us, did He undergo such an experience without turning His back and leaving. Prior to His crucifixion, Christ told His followers that where they are not accepted appropriately, they should turn and get out. Forgive, yes, but don't undergo repeated persecution unless it's for Christ's sake and for His glory.

There will be many times in situations with your family and friends where you'll deal with minor hurts, both in receiving them and in giving them. Those hurts are often the hardest to handle because they are usually unexpected from people close to you. Sincerely saying you're sorry is often incredibly difficult yet incredibly important in following Jesus.

The number one block to humbly forgiving others and asking forgiveness is pride. Pride says, "You deserve better. How can somebody treat you like this! Why should you be the one to say you're sorry!" Satan's ace in the hole is pride, and he wants to keep you stuck in it! Here's a sure cure for pride: dying to self and selfishness.

Ted never learned to say he was sorry as a child and had to really work at it when his wife pointed out this fault. Ted says, "I would think a little time would patch things up, but it usually didn't. Telling my wife and children I was sorry, however, brought rapid healing of hurt feelings and greater respect for me as a father and husband. I made it a priority to say I'm sorry and ask forgiveness. My advice is to say 'I'm sorry' and mean it."

When people tell you they're sorry and ask you to forgive them, Christ enables you to forgive by giving you the power through His grace. Otherwise, it's often simply impossible.

Grace is a gift of empowerment. Christ is ready and waiting to make you willing and capable of both forgiving yourself and others and saying you're sorry when you have been wrong.

Exploring Scripture

"I have been crucified with Christ; it is no longer I who live, but Christ lives in me; and the life which I now live in the flesh I live by faith in the Son of God, who loved me and gave Himself for me" (Galatians 2:20).

- How does Paul describe his experience of death to self in this verse?

For In-Depth Study

Read Matthew 18:21–35 where Jesus instructs the disciples in the difficult art of forgiveness. Most teachers of the law said it was only necessary the forgive a person three times. Peter goes as far as suggesting seven times which implies without limit.

- What does Jesus' answer and the parable tell us about God's attitude toward forgiveness?

- In what ways are verses 34–35 literally fulfilled today when we fail to forgive?

Taking Action

Here are six steps to help you maintain a humble spirit that can forgive and say "I'm sorry":

1. Pray for the other person's good.

2. Pray for forgiveness to be in your heart.

3. Think about how you've been forgiven by Jesus and others.

4. Read what the Bible has to say about forgiveness.

5. Make a commitment of your will to forgive even if your feelings object.

6. Be quick to admit your own weaknesses.

A regular daily time of prayer, praising and thanking God, confessing sin, and making requests of God is essential for keeping your attitude right.

- What's the best time of day for you to spend time with God?

- Are there people against whom you bear a grudge? Write their names below, tell the Lord in an audible prayer that you are releasing the hurt and anger you feel, and that you are forgiving them. Then draw a line through that name and write "forgiven" on the line.

#40 Not Copping Out

Why are talk show hosts so popular? One reason is that they have the ability and opportunity to speak out. People call shows to praise hosts for saying things they're reluctant to say personally or that others won't listen to if the caller had said it.

Dads, have you ever decided not to correct another person who was obviously deviating from God's plan because you didn't want to offend him or her? Perhaps you didn't want to risk making someone uncomfortable—a neighbor or a friend at work with whom you have a continuing relationship.

In your community, at your kid's school, or in your work, have you gotten riled up about something you knew wasn't right and then just let it pass? Isn't this a socially correct cop-out?

Today's popular, yet spiritually incorrect culture, tells you that feelings are a sacred part of who people are. It would devastate others if you confronted them with genuine honesty. It would be your fault if they got upset.

Let's checking with Jesus, our model. Jesus was always careful not to hurt people's feelings, right? Consider the following:

Was the Lord always sensitive to unbelievers' emotional tenderness?

- Did Jesus always accept without comment the opinions of others even if they were different from His own?

• If His opinion was considered politically or socially incorrect, did Jesus keep it to Himself?

The biblically correct answer is "no" on all counts.

Wouldn't Jesus be great on the evening news? The lead story might sound something like this: Today Jesus accused the Pharisees of washing themselves on the outside and being filthy on the inside like a grave that's been painted over. Representatives of the Paint and Whitewash Manufacturers Association condemned this obvious attack on their trade.

Furthermore, Jesus met privately with a woman at a well in Samaria. Reports have it that he questioned her lifestyle choices and sought to impose his own moral standards upon her. Former husband number five refused to comment, but a man who identified himself as her current companion objected to Jesus' intrusion into their private affairs. Just last week at the temple, Jesus called for an investigation into the alleged corruption of religious businesses conducted in the temple compound. The High Priest's office did not respond to our request for an interview.

Exploring Scripture

At the end of Jesus' temptation in the wilderness by Satan in Matthew 4:10, Jesus said, "Away with you, Satan! For it is written, 'You shall worship the LORD your God, and Him only you shall serve.'" Then in verse 17 we read, "From that time Jesus began to preach and to say, 'Repent, for the kingdom of heaven is at hand.'" Jesus was bold and clear. We are to worship God only and promptly repent of our sin. Period.

For In-Depth Study

Read aloud Jesus' conversations in the book of Matthew and consider the following:

- In what situations was Jesus most bold? Why?

- In what situations did Jesus choose a less confrontational approach? Why?

Taking Action

- Write down the issues that really bother you. God often allows you to experience righteous anger or indignant concern in an area where He'd like you to take action. Is He urging you to take action? Prayer is one of the most powerful things you can do when you see others violating God's laws. Commit yourself to pray each day for God to be at work in the situation.

- In addition to prayer, what steps can you actively take in the situation? Are you registered to vote? Do you write or call your elected representatives? Have you written a letter to the editor? Have you served on the school board, parents' committee, or local government board? Can you find common ground with those who may not completely agree with you? Write down three things you plan to do in response to troubling situations.

#41 Raising Spiritual Giants

Sharing your faith is the foundation for nurturing spiritual giants. Yes, you can show your Christian values through your actions, but words are important, too. Sometimes it's tough to know how to start. Sometimes it's easier to share your faith with someone outside the family than with your own children.

Many times we just need some help to get started. How about trying this example for a bedtime sharing session with your children. Bedtime always seems to be a more tender time of the day. Say something like: "[Son's or daughter's name], I want to ask you a question. Think about this carefully. What's the most thrilling experience you've ever had? Tell me what has really impressed and excited you thus far in your life? What stands out as most special?"

After they answer, say, "That's really neat. I'm glad you remember it. I want to let you in on a secret. Whatever you describe—as great as it seems now—can't compare to knowing the love of Jesus. Maybe an example can help me explain. Think of Christmas night, after all the presents were opened and our relatives were gone and we were home alone. When the excitement over your new toys dimmed a bit and tomorrow was just another day, did you feel a little sad because the celebration was all over?"

Go on to say, "Well, with Jesus, when I'm living each day for Him, the wonder and newness are always present and getting better and better. When you see people and things through His Word, through His eyes, as it were, it's like looking through a kaleidoscope of light. Everything around is the same, but different.

A little incident of joy or even pain becomes a pattern of beauty in Him and through Him."

Explain to your child, "Light is important because in the shadows or darkness you can't see clearly, right? Did you ever feel Jesus creating a warm brightness that spreads through your entire being, that sort of makes you want to stop whatever you're doing to hold on to the moment with Him? Yet even then you know there's so much more of Him, that's only a tiny fraction of His mighty person."

You might end with some promises from Scripture—"The gospel of John says that Jesus wants us to have abundant life, a life that's really satisfying. I hope you'll find that kind of life in following Jesus, too." Of course, these are all someone else's words. You'll want to use your own to give your testimony.

Exploring Scripture

In Matthew 6:22 Jesus describes the effects of light when He says, "The lamp of the body is the eye. If therefore your eye is good [that is, if you see rightly], your whole body will be full of light." When our eyes are opened to the truth, we'll never look at anything in life the same way again.

- How has God's Word changed the way you think about certain things?

Taking Action

- On a separate sheet of paper, write in your own words what Jesus means to you. Begin something like this: "Dear [Name], these are just a few thoughts about the wonderful, life-giving God I worship. I want you to be with me in Christ's presence someday because in His presence is the fullness of joy (see Psalm 16:11). I want you to know Jesus as I do."

Give a copy of what you've written to your children. Tell them to tuck it away to reread and share with your grandchildren someday.

#42 Understanding Your Origin

What does the theory of evolution have to do with being a dad and a man in command of your family?

Lots! First, consider the consequences of the theory of evolution on the self-identity of your children. How would you feel if you grew up believing that you were a chance glob of matter formed without design or purpose? The theory of evolution tells your children that they are not unique creations. It's one of the most damaging ways to attack children's self-esteem.

Teach your little ones the truth. Here is an example of what you can say. "Your existence counts for something. You're important. You're not just a chance blob, you're designed and planned and worthwhile. You have a reason to think highly of yourself. You've been made in the image and likeness of God. Your Creator has a purpose for your life. I'm going to help you live this out."

Don't count on the public schools to give the correct viewpoint here. The scientific establishment, academic community, and professional education organizations that influence the curriculum in every public school have committed themselves to upholding and promoting the theory of evolution as fact. Yet, evolution is still only an unproved theory!

Do your own research on this crucial subject and share with your children some of the amazing facts of God's creation.

Exploring Scripture

Jeremiah 29:11 says, "'For I know the thoughts that I think toward you, says the LORD, thoughts of peace and not of evil, to give you a future and a hope." You are not just gobs of some chance substance!

Encourage your children to meditate on what God has to say about them:

"Thus says the LORD, who stretches out the heavens, lays the foundation of the earth, and forms the spirit of man within him" (Zechariah 12:1).

"The Spirit Himself bears witness with our spirit that we are children of God" (Romans 8:16).

For In-Depth Study

Read Psalm 139 with your family and meditate of God's attributes.

"O LORD, You have searched me and known me.
You know my sitting down and my rising up;
You understand my thought afar off.
You have hedged me behind and before,
And laid your hand upon me.
Such knowledge is too wonderful for me;
It is high, I cannot attain it.
You have hedged me behind and before,
And laid your hand upon me.
Such knowledge is too wonderful for me;

It is high, I cannot attain it.
Where can I go from Your Spirit?
Or where can I flee from Your presence?
If I ascend into heaven, You are there;
If I make my bed in hell, behold, You are there.
If I take the wings of the morning,
And dwell in the uttermost parts of the sea,
Even there Your hand shall lead me,
And Your right hand shall hold me.
If I say, "Surely the darkness shall fall on me,"
Even the night shall be light about me;
Indeed, the darkness shall not hide from You,
But the night shines as the day;
The darkness and the light are both alike to You.
For You formed my inward parts;
You covered me in my mother's womb.
I will praise You, for I am fearfully and wonderfully made;
Marvelous are your works,
And that my soul knows very well.
My frame was not hidden from You,
When I was made in secret,
And skillfully wrought in the lowest parts of the earth.
Your eyes saw my substance, being yet unformed.
And in Your book they all were written,
The days fashioned for me,
When as yet there were none of them.
How precious also are Your thoughts to me, O God!
How great is the sum of them!
If I should count them, they would be more in number than the
sand;
When I awake, I am still with You.
Oh, that You would slay the wicked, O God!

Depart from me, therefore, you bloodthirsty men.
For they speak against You wickedly;
Your enemies take Your name in vain.
Do I not hate them, O LORD, who hate You?
And do I not loathe those who rise up against You?
I hate them with perfect hatred;
I count them my enemies.
Search me, O God, and know my heart;
Try me, and know my anxieties;
And see if there is any wicked way in me,
And lead me in the way everlasting."

Taking Action

Think about how you can communicate these truths to your children:

- Evolution is not a fact, only a theory that has not been verified.

- Each child was specially created by a loving God who knew him or her even before birth.

#43 Activating Faith

Hebrews 11:1 defines faith as "the substance of things hoped for, the evidence of things not seen." Webster's dictionary defines faith as a firm belief in something for which there is no proof. If you have faith a rock can float, it still will not stay above water. Faith that is biblical is well placed. The object of your faith must be able to perform as you expect. Biblical faith is placed in God the Father, Son and Holy Spirit.

When our son became terminally ill with cancer, we put faith in doctors alone at first. Months later when the doctors offered no hope, we started a serious study of faith. Until nothing else worked we didn't need supernatural faith.

Slowly, we began to realize that faith is an action, a commitment of the will to believe that God is in charge, that He is at work for our good, and that He likes to be taken seriously on His promises. Faith is like a muscle; it needs to be exercised. Wayne's favorite Scripture verse became Hebrews 10:23: "Let us hold fast the confession of our hope without wavering, for He who promised is faithful."

We continued to believe God would heal our son from cancer even after our son was hit by a drunk driver and even after the cancer spread through his entire body. The doctors said the end was near, but we saw the interventions of God over and over until David was completely healed following a bone marrow transplant. Was his healing from the procedure alone? Hardly. The two patients who received transplants before David and the two after him died, but David was completely healed.

Would we have lost his faith in God if God had not healed David? No! We believed God would have had a special reason for choosing not to heal, but it wouldn't be because we hadn't asked in faith and believed. Faith is an act of the will that says, "I will believe God no matter what!"

You may think you have faith, but wonder. You can know for sure. Every day you can practice faith when you pray for others or yourself. Faith is a commitment to believe that all truth and reality is not based on what you see, but on what you know to be true from God's Word.

Remember, you can keep your faith alive, active, and growing by using it. Faith can be as tiny as the head of a pin, as long as it's real. Faith is always a risk, but Jesus loves the risk-taker who is willing to put confidence in Him.

Exploring Scripture

"But without faith it is impossible to please Him, for he who comes to God must believe that He is, and that He is a rewarder of those who diligently seek Him" (Hebrews 11:6).

- We exercise faith when we believe that God exists and that He rewards us for seeking Him.
- God is pleased when we seek Him wholeheartedly.

In Matthew 21:21–22, Jesus says, "Assuredly, I say to you, if you have faith and do not doubt, you will not only do what was done to the fig tree, but also if you say to this mountain, 'Be removed and be cast into the sea,' it will be done. And whatever things you ask in prayer, believing, you will receive." Both

Matthew and Mark were impressed enough with Jesus' words to record this conversation with Him.

- What mountains do you face that need moving? Mark 6:5–6 reads, "Now He could do no mighty work there, except that He laid His hands on a few sick people and healed them. And He marveled because of their unbelief. Then He went about the villages in a circuit, teaching."

Matthew 8:10 says: "When Jesus heard it, He marveled, and said to those who followed, 'Assuredly, I say to you, I have not found such great faith, not even in Israel!'"

- What was the thing that amazed Jesus in these different situations?

Taking Action

- Share a time when you've been filled with doubt. What helped?
- Do you still struggle with a wavering in your faith?
- How has your faith been tested lately?

Record and memorize these verses:

- Mark 11:22, 24—"So Jesus answered and said to them, 'Have faith in God. . . . Therefore I say to you, whatever things you ask when you pray, believe that you receive them, and you will have them.'"
- Matthew 9:29—"'According to your faith let it be to you.'"

#44 Asking God First

Faith in God results in asking for God's help first. There's not a thing that touches your life that God does not know about. He stands ready to help you keep your promises.

When Hurricane Hugo struck Florida, many people complained that the federal government didn't come to their aid quickly enough because President Bush couldn't authorize aid immediately. Because of laws regarding states' rights, the federal government can't arbitrarily send aid until the governor of a state asks for it. Aid was ready and waiting for the asking.

We need to develop the habit of asking Jesus for help immediately, not seeking His help as a last resort. The habit of seeking God's assistance first is the greatest security we can provide our children and ourselves. God answers prayers about big things and small things. It's okay to approach Him for any kind of situation.

One Saturday Wayne decided to put up extra insulation in our basement ceiling. It was tedious work hammering nails to secure wire that supported the insulation. After one of several interruptions he couldn't find the hammer.

After a few minutes of checking all the usual places without success, Wayne prayed, "Lord, where is my hammer?" Immediately his eyes were directed to look up, and there was his hammer, suspended near the ceiling where he'd left it! Just a small item, but a reminder - ask God first no matter what the situation.

God will help in all situations, not just the big concerns. In the days of the early church, people learned to be men and women of faith by recounting the stories of how God rewarded the faith of Abraham and Moses and other biblical heroes. These accounts are worth repeating, but don't stop there. Throughout your life you're gathering together your own faith stories.

Exploring Scripture

James 5:16–17 says, "The effectual, fervent prayer of a righteous man avails much. Elijah was a man with a nature like ours, and he prayed earnestly that it would not rain; and it did not rain on the land for three years and six months."

- How do these verses cut through our common excuses for not praying?

Consider Philippians 4:6–7: "Be anxious for nothing, but in everything by prayer and supplication, with thanksgiving, let your requests be made known to God; and the peace of God, which surpasses all understanding, will guard your hearts and minds through Christ Jesus."

- What positive benefits will prayer have in our lives?

Taking Action

Discuss with your children your life of faith and answered prayers.

- Maybe you'll want to write up a brief spiritual biography.

- How has the Lord has provided for you and your family in

specific circumstances of your life? Did you have to wait sometimes?

- When was His answer was different than what you'd expected?

- When have you failed to ask God first and messed up? What do you need to ask God for right now?

- Record your prayers and the date here. Six months later come back here and write down God's answers.

#45 Developing Humility

Humility is one of those words that can best be described by saying what it's not—humility is the absence of vanity, arrogance, or haughty pride. How can you become less prideful? First, be willing. It isn't easy to squelch one's ego.

It's easy to be confused about the difference between pride and self-confidence. God expects you to be confident in using the talents He has given you. Every time I make a commitment to counsel a client, I honestly believe I'm qualified to help. Without this kind of confidence, I couldn't even begin. Yet she recognizes she's only the facilitator of wholeness—Jesus is the healer. Recognizing our ultimate dependence on Him is the essence of humility.

Wayne knows that he has strong golf and teaching skills. It's one thing to humbly recognize the God-given gifts he has developed through use and another to feel he somehow deserved or earned them. He says, "I have a healthy self-image through Christ, and a good instructor. It's okay that I'm not Jack Nicklaus or Greg Norman."

All excellence comes from Christ not from self. If it came from self, then only the physically attractive and the successful achievers would have a healthy self-image. Find your significance in what God says about you, not in what the world says. Remember, God says you're holy, blameless, beloved—worth dying for, in fact!

You may want to memorize Paul's words on this important quality of humility in Colossians 3:12. "Therefore as the elect of God, holy and beloved, put on tender mercies, kindness, humility, meekness, longsuffering." In Titus 3:2 Paul instructs Titus to remind people "to speak evil of no one, to be peaceable, gentle, showing all humility to all men."

Jesus was humble. Humble and meek are synonyms—modest, submissive, not overly concerned with being important. You'll nurture humility in yourself and others as you remember that every Christian is gifted in some way by God—not by self—and can have a positive impact.

Underlying giftedness comes from Christ. Sure, it takes work to develop that giftedness, but your basic ability comes from God and is intended to honor Him. It's helpful to associate with humble people. Romans 12:16 says, "Be of the same mind toward one another. Do not set your mind on high things, but associate with the humble. Do not be wise in your own opinion."

Be wary of linking job descriptions or level of income with your value. God said this about the craftsmen who built the tabernacle: "I have filled him with the Spirit of God, in wisdom, in understanding, in knowledge, and in all kinds of workmanship. . . . I have put wisdom in the hearts of all the gifted artisans, that they may make all that I have commanded you" (Exodus 31:3, 6).

Exploring Scripture

"Let another man praise you, and not your own mouth; a stranger, and not your own lips" (Proverbs 27:2). Don't blow your own horn! Remember, God values humility.

Can you think of examples when the following verses have proven true?

- Job 22:29—"When they cast you down, and you say, 'Exaltation will come!' then He will save the humble person."

- Job 5:11—"He sets on high those who are lowly."

As a merciful but just Being, God has unpleasant consequences for those who violate His principle of humility. Notice how God deals with the proud person.

- 1 Peter 5:5—"God resists the proud, but gives grace to the humble."

Matthew 23:12—"And whoever exalts himself will be humbled, and he who humbles himself will be exalted."

Proverbs 3:34—"Surely He scorns the scornful, but gives grace to the humble."

Taking Action

- On separate sheets of paper make a list of the God-given gifts you see in yourself, your spouse, in each of your children, and your grandchildren.

- Is there an area of expertise in your life where you've hogged the credit and not given credit to God? If so, write it down as a reminder.

- In what area(s) of your life do you find it most difficult to be humble? Meditate on God's blessings upon the humble, and remind yourself of His strong warnings against pride.

- Who do you know who fits the description of a humble person?

#46 Experiencing God Personally

Scripture is packed with accounts of people's experiences with God. Some men shy away from the thought of an "experience" with God because they believe a faith that is based on "an experience of God" is "emotional" and therefore second-rate. Now God never wants you to put your brain on a shelf, but neither are you to put your feelings on a shelf.

Peter and the other apostles were dramatically changed by their personal contacts with Jesus. Paul had a life-changing experience with the Lord one day that challenged his previously ironclad belief system.

Who's the last man you saw talking to a burning bush? Can you believe someone could have a radiant expression while being stoned to death? Moses and Stephen had these powerful personal experiences with God.

God uses unusual methods at times to get our attention? Sure— God can do anything. But don't expect these dramatic experiences to be the only real sign of God's presence in your life. What is He doing in and through your life right now?

Be willing to meet the Lord in regular Bible study and prayer. You may have an experience like the two men had on the road to Emmaus (Luke 24:13–35). As they were with Jesus, they gradually came to an understanding of who Jesus was and what His words meant, and their faith was encouraged.

Don't expect God to work like a tool and die-maker filling molds. He gives everyone a unique experience of Himself. For one person this encounter may be low-key; for another, more intense. For some it's a dramatic insight or startling answer to prayer; for others it's a steadily growing awareness, day in, day out.

Remember, God loved the other Israelites no less than Moses when He led them out of Egypt. But the other Israelites didn't see all the miraculous signs God showed Moses. If someone tells you they had a special encounter with God, don't write them off as crazy. Time will tell if their encounter with God changes their life or not. Just because someone experiences God a certain way doesn't mean you or the rest of the world will or should have the same experience.

What's most important is to always seek more of God. Here are simple steps to take to encounter God personally in your life.

- Let your daily prayer be, "God, I want to know you better. Show me, teach me."

- Meditate on the Psalms. Every emotion you'll ever experience about God is described there.

- Seek God through His creation. Spend some time outdoors every day appreciating the gift of His world.

- When you're with other believers, expect to see reflections of Him in others.

Set up your own customized program for reading Scripture each day; begin with one verse or one chapter. Think about what you're reading. Ask God to show you something new that you never knew about Him or His ways. Take time to listen to what God tells you through His Word!

Exploring Scripture

Study Moses' experiences with God at the start of his ministry in Exodus 2–4.

Study Stephen's experience of God at his death as recorded in Acts 7:54–60.

"When they heard these things they were cut to the heart, and they gnashed at him with their teeth. But he, being full of the Holy Spirit, gazed into heaven and saw the glory of God, and Jesus standing at the right hand of God, and said, "Look! I see the heavens opened and the Son of Man standing at the right hand of God!"

Then they cried out with a loud voice, stopped their ears, and ran at him with one accord; and they cast him out of the city and stoned him. And the witnesses laid down their clothes at the feet of a young man named Saul.

And they stoned Stephen as he was calling on God and saying, "Lord Jesus, receive my spirit." Then he knelt down and cried out with a loud voice, "Lord, do not charge them with this sin." And when he had said this, he fell asleep.

- What was it in Stephen's experience with God that gave him the boldness to speak as he did?

Taking Action

Many churches encourage weekly small groups during which men share their moments closest to Christ, their prayers, study, and actions. This encourages men to be constantly alert to experiencing God each week. Might you be able to participate?

- When was your moment closest to Christ this week? Tell somebody about it.

#47 Surviving the Impossible

When you're wiped out, washed up, and done for? You've tried everything; you've nothing left to give; you're totally desperate. Just when you think you're finally going to make it through, more trouble hits. Things go from bad to worse. What do you do? Is there a way when it seems like there is no way?

A corporation Wayne had worked for was acquired in a merger. What Wayne had considered a secure future was suddenly in jeopardy. On one day's notice, the new CEO asked Wayne to present the perfect sales presentations on the company's product line to twenty-five regional managers. Marketing, not sales, was Wayne's area of expertise, and he had only a couple hours that night to prepare for the 9 a.m. meeting.

Wayne prayed and worked until 4 a.m. The situation seemed hopeless; nothing was coming together. Visions ran rampant in his head. "I'll blow this and lose my job for sure." After a few hours sleep, Wayne got up, still unprepared.

Wayne was totally discouraged and exhausted when he walked into that morning meeting. The CEO pulled Wayne aside and said he had changed his mind and hoped Wayne wouldn't be upset if they didn't use his presentations! God helped Wayne survive what seemed to be an impossible situation! Not with help in preparation for the sales presentation, but by eliminating the need to do it at all!

First, get past the "why am I in this difficult situation." God never promised a world without pain, only an eternity of joy.

Don't consider your circumstances uncommon. Instead, concentrate on these certainties:

- God knows what's happening.

- God allows what's happening.

- God works in what's happening.

Next, look for any area where your life might be out of order or displeasing to the Lord. If there are issues that need to be dealt with, make them right with the Lord. Then consider if there's something God is trying to teach you through your situation. Ask Him to reveal any lesson He wants you to learn.

Even if everything that you hold of value is lost, don't forget that God still has a plan for you. Wait for the Lord with confidence no matter what you see in the immediate situation. And when the trouble has passed, thank God and tell others what He has done for you! Honor God by talking about His goodness and His help.

Exploring Scripture

1 Peter 4:12–13 says, "Beloved do not think it strange concerning the fiery trial which is to try you, as though some strange thing happened to you; but rejoice to the extent that you partake of Christ's sufferings, that when His glory is revealed, you may also be glad with exceeding joy."

- How did Peter understand suffering as a part of the Christian's experience?

- What encouragement does this give you when you go through suffering?

For In-Depth Study

Psalm 107 is about how God met the need of the lost, the lonely, the endangered, and the discouraged. Verse 43 says, "Whoever is wise will observe these things, and they will understand the lovingkindness of the LORD." In Psalm 107 you'll find many examples and reasons we are to praise God's goodness even in suffering.

Taking Action

- Describe tough times you've faced in the past. How did you handle it?

- How have those experiences affected your walk with the Lord?

- If you are facing this kind of tough time now, how might you deal with it better?

#48 Controlling the Food Monster

An area of potential sneaky sinfulness that is often overlooked is diet. Men who are free from serious sin in other areas of their lives often succumb to the seemingly innocent indulgence of overeating. Making poor food choices harms your body, the temple of the Holy Spirit.

Why do men do this?

- Food as a reward? (I don't do other sinful things, so I deserve to go overboard on food)

- Food as comfort? (Covering up loneliness, hurt, disappointment)

- Food as substitute for a satisfying sex life? (Needing emotional and sexual intimacy)

During childhood men establish their own system of rewards and comfort. Food or drink is often the escape of choice because food or drink never talks back, never complains, never nags, and, of course, tastes good. These men failed to find positive reinforcement as an adult by expressing their needs to other nurturing adults.

A vicious cycle can set in. From overeating or drinking, lack of exercise, or overwork many men develop poor health and lose the ability and energy to have fun with their families. This increases a man's emotional distance from his children and eventually decreases his wife's desire for sexual intimacy.

What's the answer?

Examine your thoughts about food and exercise. Exercise of any kind can increase energy, decrease the desire for food, and facilitate weight loss. If you don't have a sport you enjoy, simply try walking more and sitting in front of the TV less. Walking can be done anywhere, anytime, and it provides a great opportunity for spousal conversation essential to developing emotional intimacy.

Exploring Scripture

First Corinthians 6:19 says, "Or do you not know that your body is the temple of the Holy Spirit who is in you, whom you have from God, and you are not your own?"

- How should this passage affect your view of health and physical fitness?

For In-Depth Study

Look up the following verses and consider how our use and misuse of food and physical appetites is presented not only as a health issue but as a spiritual issue as well:

Matthew 6:25–33
John 4:31–34
Romans 14:1–12
1 Corinthians 10:31–33
1 Timothy 5:7–8

Taking Action

You have the knowledge, responsibility, and capability to choose healthful food. Heart disease, stroke, cancer, and even minor infections are clearly affected by diet.

Take this food quiz by answering yes or no.

_____ Do your food choices demonstrate your self-discipline?

_____ Does what you eat demonstrate to your wife and kids, "I want to be around a long time to enjoy you"?

_____ What changes do you need to make in your diet?

_____ What exercises would make your body healthier?

_____ What's keeping you from developing these good habits?

_____ Whom can you ask to hold you accountable to follow through in keeping your promises to maintain healthy eating habits?

#49 Maintaining Integrity

Integrity is more than being honest. It means "being whole and complete, no disparate parts, no elements out of balance." Balance is a key factor in maintaining integrity. Sometimes a man becomes a different "self" in his business than he is at home, a different "self" on the golf course than he is in church. Separate, external fronts become facades of who the man really is. Ultimately they cause confusion and division between the inner and outer person. Furthermore, being a different person or "self" on different occasions can make it difficult for a man to resist temptation. Be authentic!

There was never a divided self in Jesus. He's the supreme example of integrity, wholeness, balance. That needs to be your goal also. Let there be only one essence of you, only one "self," and maintain the same consistency in behavior, values, and beliefs that's part of you now and will be present in the future, too—at home, work, in recreation, in worship, and in all your relationships.

The Word of God contains all the principles you need to achieve wholeness—one integrated "self." For example, the Word teaches you how to deal with anger. Inappropriate or uncontrollable anger damages your integrity as well as hinders your witness in your family, at work, and in recreational settings. Don't let uncontrollable outbursts of anger be dictated by situations or by other people.

Sometimes it may seem like your strong religious convictions make you a ready target for these situations. People may deliberately try to get you to go against your values. Responding impulsively can damage your ability to maintain your integrity and your inner harmony—your one consistent "self"—as well as your Christian witness.

Exploring Scripture

"He who is slow to wrath has great understanding, but he who is impulsive exalts folly" (Proverbs 14:29).

• What does an impulsive emotional response lead to?

"A wrathful man stirs up strife, but he who is slow to anger allays contention" (Proverbs 15:18). "So then, my beloved brethren, let every man be swift to hear, slow to speak, slow to wrath" (James 1:19).

• What problems can be avoided according, to these two verses?

For In-Depth Study

As a man of integrity, sometimes you'll need to disregard what people say about you. In Matthew 22:16 it is said of Jesus, "Teacher, we know that You are true, and teach the way of God in truth; nor do You care about anyone, for You do not regard the person of men."

Read the context of this passage in Matthew 22:15–22 and determine why we need to use discernment even in accepting compliments.

Run this idea past your children who may someday struggle to be accepted by peers because of their faith.

Taking Action

Most of us who have "been around the block once or twice" know that some individuals in the world can be vicious. Study God's Word by yourself with a guide such as this book, but it's also helpful to pursue integrity and growth as a husband and father in a support community of men. You can usually best maintain integrity if you're part of a buddy system.

Find a like-minded man or group of men with whom to associate. Remember, Jesus discipled a group. There's a dynamic in a group interaction that can't be duplicated when we're by ourselves. There are excellent men's retreats and conventions designed to help men develop integrity.

We all need inspiration from thoughtful messages and the encouragement of other men. In these meetings men hold one another accountable to be godly husbands and fathers. If you've shied away from group experiences in the past, you may wish to try again now. Check out a few until you find a group you're comfortable with. It's worth the effort.

#50 Showing You Care

Someday, far more quickly than you think possible, the children who seemed as if they'd be part of your household forever will have grown up and be on their own. You'll still care just as much about them. Show it! Call your grown sons or daughters at home or even at work occasionally. Make breakfast or lunch dates if they live close by or even a short drive away. Plan convenient times to be together for extended conversations.

During these conversations ask personal questions like:

- Are you satisfied with your work?

- How's it really going?

- What are you doing to improve your relationship with Jesus?

- Are you satisfied with your spiritual growth?

- How are things with you and your spouse?

These are the really important areas of their lives; talk about them! You'll need to get beyond the surface chatter to stay current and involved in their lives.

Why? Because your children still need you, whatever their ages. They need your maturity and the wisdom to be gained from your years of experience. The job of parenting doesn't come with a retirement package!

Celebrate special days—school successes, anniversaries, birthdays—with your spouse, children, and parents. Send notes out of the blue reminding your children how much you love them.

How about sharing your own struggles to maintain your Christian integrity at work? Or asking your children's advice occasionally? We've learned much from our older children. Often their perception of a problem is both accurate and full of insight. Share some of the material in this study with older children, gearing it to their ages, and watch the results.

Don't make your wife the only contact person with adult children. Does this sound familiar?

Too often a husband asks his wife, "Have you talked to the kids? What did they say? How are they doing?"

Maybe you made some mistakes, and your kids have already pulled away. We've seen God soften children's memories of harshness or indifference from their dads, especially when grown children experience signs of parental love later. Remember, deep down in their hearts, your children always want to make it right with you. However old they grow, they still want your approval. Try showing it even if they're stiff and standoffish at first. They may be testing your sincerity. Don't quit. God has healed the past for countless people.

If your parents are still living, how's your relationship with them? Often adult children are able to talk through previously painful issues with their older parents.

Be non-condemning but honest. Say things like, "I'm sure you didn't want to hurt me, but I really felt bad when. . . ." Even a previously damaged relationship can be repaired, dads, either with your children or with your own parents. The important thing is to never stop showing you care.

Exploring Scripture

Read about the prodigal son in Luke 15:11–32. Then He said: "A certain man had two sons. And the younger of them said to his father, 'Father, give me the portion of goods that falls to me.' So he divided to them his livelihood. And not many days after, the younger son gathered all together, journeyed to a far country, and there wasted his possessions with prodigal living. But when he had spent all, there arose a severe famine in that land, and he began to be in want.

Then he went and joined himself to a citizen of that country, and he sent him into his fields to feed swine. And he would gladly have filled his stomach with the pods that the swine ate, and no one gave him anything. But when he came to himself, he said, 'How many of my father's hired servants have bread enough and to spare, and I perish with hunger! 'I will arise and go to my father, and will say to him, "Father, I have sinned against heaven and before you, and I am no longer worthy to be called your son. Make me like one of your hired servants."'

And he arose and came to his father. But when he was still a great way off, his father saw him and had compassion, and ran and fell on his neck and kissed him. And the son said to him, 'Father, I have sinned against heaven and in your sight, and am no longer worthy to be called your son.' But the father said to his servants, 'Bring out the best robe and put it on him, and put a ring on his hand and sandals on his feet. And bring the fatted calf here and kill it, and let us eat and be merry; for this my son was dead and is alive again; he was lost and is found.' And they began to be merry.

Now his older son was in the field. And as he came and drew near to the house, he heard music and dancing. So he called one of the servants and asked what these things meant. And he said to him, 'Your brother has come, and because he has received him safe and sound, your father has killed the fatted calf.' But he was angry and would not go in.

Therefore his father came out and pleaded with him. So he answered and said to his father, 'Lo, these many years I have been serving you; I never transgressed your commandment at any time; and yet you never gave me a young goat, that I might make merry with my friends. But as soon as this son of yours came, who has devoured your livelihood with harlots, you killed the fatted calf for him.' And he said to him, 'Son, you are always with me, and all that I have is yours. It was right that we should make merry and be glad, for your brother was dead and is alive again, and was lost and is found.'"

Write up a profile of the prodigal, the father, and the elder brother. How did the father deal with each son and why? What lessons does this provide for your own parent/child relationships?

Taking Action

- Consider your own young adult years. What unresolved issues remain between you and your parents that need to be forgiven? Write down your plan to seek forgiveness from them and to forgive others who have hurt you.

Have your children taken the prodigal road away from home? List their names and a specific way you can show them you love them and will always be there for them.

#51 Being a Grandpa

You may be privileged to influence another generation of your offspring—your grandchildren. Being a grandparent is the parenting opportunity again in new form. It's second in importance only to being a dad. You can have an impact not only on your grandchildren but also on your grown sons and daughters as they watch and learn your style of relating to and training children.

The twentieth and twenty-first centuries may be very different technologically, but the basic needs of kids and grandkids won't change. We see this in our own family. What our grandkids want are time and attention from someone who's crazy about them as only a parent or a grandparent can be, somebody who's willing to set aside part of his or her personal life to be with them. Parents can be so busy! So are grandparents; but they've learned the importance of stopping for the significant opportunities of life, and they often have more flexible schedules.

Settle your grandchild on your lap and tell your own made-up stories. Just start talking about Peter the Pumpkin-Eater or whatever your imagination dreams up. Watch little eyes light up as they listen. You'll soon understand what it means to spin a yarn, never knowing where you'll end when you begin. Children especially like it when you include them in a story by name.

Wayne likes to tell his own made-up stories to our grandchildren, but he also reads stories to them often using a big book of Bible stories. He never learned the Bible stories as a child and is finally getting all the Old Testament stories straight.

Your grown children, when they're parents themselves, will need time for a dinner out for uninterrupted conversation with their spouses. If you live nearby, you can babysit occasionally but don't overdo it because you don't have the primary responsibility of parents. Be sure your adult children realize this. Teach them to parent by the principles that you have learned from God's Word.

Exploring Scripture

Psalm 127:3–4 says, "Behold, children are a heritage from the LORD, the fruit of the womb is a reward. Like arrows in the hand of a warrior, so are the children of one's youth."

- How is the view of contemporary society in regards to children and that of the Bible different?

    Matthew 18:5–6 says, "Whoever receives one little child like this in My name receives Me.

    But whoever causes one of these little ones who believe in Me to sin, it would be better for him if a millstone were hung around his neck, and he were drowned in the depth of the sea."

- How would you summarize this passage's warning about the importance of our influence on the lives of children?

Taking Action

During all your special moments with your children and grandchildren, you can shape your family history for generations to come by making sure your offspring:

- know God

- desire to honor Him

- do all things for His glory

Plan at each family gathering (Thanksgiving, Christmas, summer vacations) to communicate to everyone your desire to see your family continue in Christian growth and maturity.

#52 Not Looking Back

Maybe you're reading this study and patting yourself on the back. On the whole you've done pretty well in balancing the responsibilities of marriage and family life. You've developed a close relationship with your wife and your children and you're growing in your relationship to the Lord—keep it up!

Perhaps you would like to work harder on your relationship with your wife, showing her a greater sense of respect and commitment. The promises that you made to her on your wedding day have become more important to you, and you want to honor them with all your heart.

Maybe you're seeing certain areas of fatherly responsibility you've mishandled or neglected for a long time. You remember how you felt looking at that small infant in the hospital nursery, how you wanted to care for, protect, and love that little gift from God. Now you feel motivated to renew those silent promises you made back then.

Perhaps your children are grown and far away from you physically, emotionally, and spiritually. Maybe you've messed up royally, and you feel discouraged. This book is intended to encourage, not to condemn. You did the best you could with what you knew at the time, but now you have a new sense of what is possible in the remaining years of life.

One of salvation's best gifts to men is that God's grace not only saves from the penalty of sinfulness but also frees men from the human compulsion to look back and berate themselves for former failures or inadequacies. When you fully grasp the depth of God's love for you in Christ Jesus and the extent of His forgiveness, it's not necessary to wallow in remorse. The Scriptures say that God has "cast all our sins into the depths of the sea" (Micah 7:19). If that's what God has done, you don't have any business conducting underwater salvage operations!

Now is the time to look toward the future rather than looking back. By His grace and through His power, you can be a man, a husband, and a father in command who keeps his promises.

Exploring Scripture

"As far as the east is from the west, so far has He removed our transgressions from us" (Psalm 103:12).

"But You have lovingly delivered my soul from the pit of corruption, for You have cast all my sins behind Your back" (Isaiah 38:17).

"He will again have compassion on us, and will subdue our iniquities. You will cast all our sins into the depths of the sea" (Micah 7:19).

"Brethren, I do not count myself to have apprehended; but one thing I do, forgetting those things which are behind and reaching forward to those things which are ahead, I press toward the goal for the prize of the upward call of God in Christ Jesus" (Philippians 3:13–14).

- How do these Scriptures give you confidence for the future?

Taking Action

Make a list of the ways in which you feel you have failed as a man, a husband, or a father. On one side of the paper, list the things you've confessed to the Lord before that still make you feel unworthy.

Write in bold letters across that side of the page,

"FORGOTTEN BY GOD."

On the other side of the paper, list the things that have occurred to you as you've worked through this book.

Across this list write in bold letters, "FORGIVEN AND FOR-GOTTEN BY GOD." The next time a sense of unworthiness hits you, remind yourself of those two words—forgiven and forgotten.

Then write:

FROM THIS DAY FORWARD I WILL BE A MAN IN COM-MAND and under the command of Almighty God.

One of the most powerful things you can ever do for your children and grandchildren is to pray for them each and every day. Prayer changes lives like words and actions alone never can. Pray for God's healing touch on any areas of your child's development that went wrong for whatever reason. Look forward expectantly. The best is yet to come!

Thanks for reading…would you be so kind as to leave a review?

We appreciate your reading Man in Command, How to Be A Great Husband and Dad. If you found these principles helpful please consider leaving a brief review to encourage other readers on Amazon at this book's page.

<u>Other Books by Dr. Judith Rolfs available on Amazon</u>:

Directive 99, adult suspense novel

Bullet In The Night, a mystery novel

52 Ways To Keep Your Promises As A Husband and Father

Loving Every Minute, 52 Ways To Live, Laugh & Love As a Woman

Love Always, Mom, A real miracle story

Triumphing Over Cancer, A Patient & Caregiver's Manual of Encouragement

Breathless Devotional Mini-Meditations for Connecting Your Heart With God's

God Thoughts, Devotions For Every Day

Soaring As A Parent, Secrets To Being Great

Secrets To Being A Super Grandparent

Joyful Christmas Reflections

For Children:

The Adventures of Tommy Smurlee

Tommy Smurlee and the Missing Statue

Hey, I've Got ADHD, Here's How You Can Help

Hey, I've Got Cancer, Here's How You Can Help

Truth for Teens, Answers to Life's Tough Questions

Unforgettable Stories For Kids

Dr. Judith Rolfs, a licensed marriage and family counselor for over twenty-five years, is a respected author of books designed to enrich family life. Follow her blog at www.judithrolfs.blogspot. com and visit her website at www.judithrolfs.com.

More Information About the Authors

Dr. Judith Rolfs has written numerous books on family issues and several mystery novels including a children's fiction series teaching positive morals. She has a B.A. in Psychology, M.S. and Ph.D. in Counseling and Guidance. Years of working with parents and children and raising their own four children and grand-parenting seven make Rolfs uniquely qualified to share her knowledge.

Her parenting courses and workshops were often co-led with her husband Wayne. Together they dealt with the family challenges that led to the development and teaching of these effective strategies for handling the common issues every family faces.

Wayne followed a successful career in the business world as a former Vice President of Puritan Industries in Chicago, with entering the golf profession and becoming a Class A PGA Pro. He has directed youth and adult golf camps and schools for the past twenty-five years. Wayne taught golf while motivating children to become the best they can be both on and off the golf course. He's also the author of The 10-30 Power Swing helping golfers hit the long ball.

Made in the USA
Columbia, SC
27 September 2022

67811160R00093